CW00447874

# *A Biblical Anthropology*

# A Biblical Anthropology
## Michael Bieleski

Published 2014
*Mishma Publications*

ISBN 978-0-473-27570-9

Copyright ©2014 Michael Bieleski

All rights reserved. This book or any portion thereof may not be reproduced or used in any manner whatsoever without the express written permission of the publisher except for the use of brief quotations in a book review or scholarly journal.

Every effort has been made to acknowledge copyrighted material quoted in this book. Every effort has been to ensure that the material included in this book follows the guidelines of fair dealing. The author apologies for any cases where appropriate permission has not been sought and if notified, will formally seek permission at the earliest opportunity.

First Printing: 2014


ISBN 978-0-473-27570-9

## Scripture References

**NRSV**- Revised Standard Version of the Bible, copyright 1952 [2nd edition, 1971] by the Division of Christian Education of the National Council of the Churches of Christ in the United States of America. Used by permission. All rights reserved

**NKJV**- Scripture taken from the New King James Version. Copyright © 1982 by Thomas Nelson, Inc. Used by permission. All rights reserved

**ESV** -Scripture quotations are from The Holy Bible, English Standard Version® (ESV®), copyright © 2001 by Crossway, a publishing ministry of Good News Publishers. Used by permission. All rights reserved

**NASB** -Scripture taken from the NEW AMERICAN STANDARD BIBLE®, Copyright © 1960,1962,1963,1968,1971,1972,1973,1975,1977,1995 by The Lockman Foundation. Used by permission

**NIV**- THE HOLY BIBLE, NEW INTERNATIONAL VERSION®, NIV® Copyright © 1973, 1978, 1984, 2011 by Biblica, Inc.™ Used by permission. All rights reserved worldwide.

**NLT**-Scripture quotations marked (NLT) are taken from the Holy Bible, New Living Translation, copyright © 1996, 2004, 2007 by Tyndale House Foundation. Used by permission of Tyndale House Publishers, Inc., Carol Stream, Illinois 60188. All rights reserved.

**NCV**-Scripture taken from the New Century Version. Copyright © 2005 by Thomas Nelson, Inc. Used by permission. All rights reserved.

Cover Illustration: Gustave Doré (1832-1883)-Public Domain

With grateful thanks to my wife Yvonne,
For her unwavering support.

# Contents

*Acknowledgement*

I am very grateful to Rev Dr Paul Prestidge who helped proof read and suggested changes where required.

# *Foreword*

The content of this book concerns the central religious questions of life-after-death, salvation and judgment, and whether the Christian scriptures present a cohesive view about these matters. It's an enormous topic that has implications for virtually every aspect of human existence. In this book Michael approaches matters in a very biblically foundational way. He's addressing evangelical Christians who, perhaps like himself, have assumed that conventional wisdom about immortal souls, eternal punishment, and the destiny of the righteous is a settled matter of biblical orthodoxy. Instead, this book demonstrates how theology can become captive to deep-seated cultural ideas, even when Scripture presents a consistently contrary view. The great strength of this book is the way Michael clearly and straightforwardly works through the relevant themes, along with the associated key scriptures, highlighting the dominant threads, while not neglecting apparently more difficult passages.

As with Michael's own journey, I hope that this book helps others re-consider what the Bible has to say about these vital issues of life and death. As Christians grasp a more cohesive and biblically faithful understanding of these matters, my hope is that the church will be able to offer the world a more convincing and powerful account of the Good News we share in Christ. In this task I hope Michael's book may be a great help to many.

Rev Dr Paul Prestidge

# *Introduction*

There have been many different types and aspects of anthropological studies, exploring the human condition in multiple ways. This book attempts to examine the metaphysical nature of man in relationship to existential issues, an area that has often been a catalyst for significant debate. For example, the dualistic approach that views body and soul as separable, contrasted with a belief in monism that treats both as inseparable elements of man.

Whatever ideas are formed will influence our understanding of man's relationship with death. Importantly, not being dead is a good thing and I can normally tell this by realising that I can think about the fact that I am thinking about this. The philosopher said, "I doubt, therefore I think, therefore I am."[1] It was a defined proof for existence based on the premise that states, because I wonder whether I exist then I must actually exist. While the premise only served to prove that the mind exists, it does demonstrate how reflection on existence influenced the way in which humans explored and defined humanity.

This process of reflection on the nature of man's existence also incorporated ideas about man's

---

[1] René Descartes, http://en.wikipedia.org/wiki/Ren%C3%A9_Descartes

mortality, because that was seen to interrupt existence. For example, ceremonial burial practices, possibly demonstrate that only man is acutely aware of his own mortality. Therefore, the generally held view is that "There is no indication that individuals of any species other than man know that they will inevitably die."[2]

*"One time Old Man said to Old Woman, "People will never die."*

*"Oh!" said Old Woman, "that will never do; because, if people live always, there will be too many people in the world."*

*"Well," said, Old Man, "we do not want to die forever. We shall die for four days and then come to life again."*

*"Oh, no!" said Old Woman, "it will be better to die forever, so that we shall be sorry for each other."*

*"Well," said Old Man, "we will decide this way. We will throw a buffalo chip into the water. If it sinks, we will die forever; if it floats, we shall live again."*

*"Well," said Old Woman, "throw it in."*

---

[2] Dobzhansky, et al, "What About Animal Consciousness?" by Brad Harrub, Ph.D.
http://www.apologeticspress.org/apcontent.aspx?category=9&article=639

*Now, Old Woman had great power, and she caused the chip
to turn into a stone, so it sank. So when we die, we die
forever."[3]*

This story from the Blackfoot Indians is predictably fatalistic about life and death. The problem of death was central to many cultural stories, and its impact unavoidable. Therefore, man has sought to define himself in the light of his own mortality, and this was often exemplified in the way that cultural systems attempted to provide a meaningful response to existential issues.

However, philosophical speculation or a culture's view of self and existence may not provide us with a complete answer. What can we hope for in terms of a suitable answer to man's problem of existence? For our purposes, the Biblical story is the most satisfactory solution to existential problems, because it contains "those documents which reflect what God desired to have recorded, in order that his purposes might be served."[4]

Therefore, our biblical anthropology will be formed around what Scripture has to say about the nature of man, death and a few other things. The fact that death is at the forefront of the Biblical message is

---

[3] Lark Wissler and D. C. Duvall, Mythology of the Blackfoot Indians (New York: Anthropological Papers of the American Museum of Natural History, 1908), v. 2, part 1, 21
[4] Stanley Grenz, Theology for the Community of God (Eerdmans), 382

exemplified in the life, death, and resurrection of Jesus Christ. To understand the mission of Jesus, "death must be recognised as the context into which the Gospels speak."[5]

Understanding what Scripture has to say about life and death, must consider any assumption that everything we know about these issues has already been settled. Many seem to share a particular and traditional view - as many an afterlife "Peter at the Pearly Gates" joke would testify. There is a heaven and a hell. The good people die and go to heaven. The bad people go to hell.

However, things are not quite that simple. While such ideas might be the general view of many, it is not necessarily what all believe. Therefore, the possibility of different views on man's metaphysical nature in this life and in death will form a key focus of this book.

Considering all these issues, it should be no surprise that the beginning of the Bible presents a detailed narrative of the dilemma of life and death. Genesis provides a quick introduction on how the world came to be, a short account of the creation of life, a detailed explanation of man's responsibilities, his failure to obey God and the outcome of that disobedience.

The narrative provides a clear explanation of man's state of existence. God created man, everything

---

[5] Tony Wright, Churchman 122/2 (Church Society) 107

was good, man sinned, and everything was now bad. Man lost his home, favour with God, and most importantly his life. Having been granted existence, that existence was to be taken away. The nature of existence as God gave, and the existence that is the outcome of man's sinful rebellion, becomes the focus of our inquiry. What future existence is there for man, and what will it look like?

To understand these issues, common principles of interpretation become essential in forming sensible beliefs. In addition, these principles are useful in understanding how Scripture itself contributes to the process of interpretation. For example, recognising difficult passages for which multiple versions of interpretation might exist helps to establish the very nature and purpose of interpretive principles. Therefore, it is important that the overall emphasis of Scripture must be understood and applied in context, rather than relying on obscure passages and isolated interpretations.

The role of man's reflection on his circumstances, and any possible contribution to the way in which God's purposes were expressed, also becomes important. Recognising the mechanisms by which man has endeavoured to understand himself in his relationship with God, will help clarify the historical processes leading to the formation of Scripture.[6] These

---

[6] Grenz, Community of God, 384

ideas will help contribute to our understanding that, "what the text meant and what it means are inseparably linked."[7]

Take for example the creation narrative and the fall of man, which is a story with special trees and a talking snake. The way in which these stories are understood is important, because while the New Testament writers reflect on the content of Genesis, they do not seem concerned about the more unusual elements of the stories.

For example, Paul could say, "I am afraid that just as Eve was deceived by the serpent's cunning, your minds may somehow be led astray from your sincere and pure devotion to Christ."[8] However, the account of Eve's deception in Genesis describes the serpent as a wild crafty animal that can talk.[9] Later on, he was cursed by God to spend the rest of his days slithering around in the dust.[10] [11] In the very next verse in Genesis 3:15 the serpent is mentioned, in what has been seen by both Catholic and Evangelical tradition,[12] as a messianic promise. "I will put enmity between you and

---

[7] Bevard Childs, Biblical Theology in Crisis (Philadelphia; Westminister, 1970) 141 quoted in Grenz, Community of God, 385
[8] 2 Corinthians 11:3 (NIV)
[9] Gen 3.1
[10] Gen 3.14
[11] In the legends of the Jews it says that the Angels from heaven came down and chopped off his hands and feet and his cries of anguish could be heard right around the world. Louis Ginzberg, (The Legends of the Jews, Jewish Publication Society of America, Philadelphia, 1973), 78
[12] Claus Westermann, Genesis 1-11, A Commentary, (Augsburg Publishing House, Minneapolis 1974), 260

the woman, and between your offspring and hers; he will crush your head, and you will strike his heel."[13]

The more unusual elements of this story, describing Satan as a crafty talking wild animal cursed to slither around in the dust, requires special consideration. This is because there is evidence of a clear etiological motif, which explains the way in which the serpent moves and feeds itself, and it belongs "to the very common myths and stories which tell how certain animals acquire their peculiar characteristics."[14] Therefore, it is apparent that there is a "mingling of history and story that is quite diverse and at times peculiar and yet the distinction between story and history is for the careful observer to discern."[15]

What might affect our ability to make the distinction between story and history, are our particular beliefs in methods of revelation or inspiration. Therefore, any attempts to reconcile the more unusual elements, requires a consideration of a systematic approach considering a range of issues, which may not be easily reconciled with a fundamentalist theology.

Within this cycle of reflection, the use of original language words understood within the original context becomes essential in establishing meaning and patterns of thought. While this book does not claim to provide a

---

[13] Genesis 3:15 (NIV)
[14] Hermann Gunkel, quoted in Westermann, Genesis 1-11, 259
[15] Gunkel, The Stories of Genesis (Bibal Press 1994), 19

comprehensive list of all supporting references, it does intend to provide a hermeneutical framework that exemplifies the overall teaching of Scripture.

In this book, we are considering a Biblical Anthropology - past, present and future. What does Scripture say about man's existence? What is man's metaphysical construction, and how does this affect our understanding of his condition? Whatever ideas we form from these questions, will become useful in clarifying Scripture's central themes, and help to explain the hope that lies ahead for man.

# *Death*

Death is a fact of life that most would find difficult to ignore and even more difficult to avoid. Certainly, no one can circumvent death although some might have tried. Recent scientific research has demonstrated, that while certain enzymes might limit the deterioration of DNA strands, this dramatically increases the chance of cancer.

Whatever way it is viewed and in whatever form it takes, death is an unpleasant thing. The actual moment of death depends on a number of factors. It is possible to resuscitate the body from clinical death,[16] although the brain can rarely survive more than 3 minutes at body temperatures. Controlled clinical death is sometimes used during operations when the heart and lungs are temporarily stopped. It is also possible for patients to be on life support systems, even though the brain is dead. In this case, the patient can be considered legally dead. Because of these variables, death is recognised as a series of physical events that begins with clinical death. Once the biological processes fully cease to function and the body begins to decompose, it is impossible to bring back the dead.

One of the useful things about Scripture is that it

---

[16] Clinical death is the cessation of breathing and circulation.

provides a clear picture of why man exists and why he dies. In the beginning, God created man and woman, placed them in a garden, and gave them responsibility for its care. In this garden, there were two specific trees, the Tree of Life, and the Tree of the Knowledge of Good and Evil. These two trees then became the central feature of an unfolding dichotomy between the temptation of rebellion and the reward of obedience. Adam and Eve were free to eat from any tree in the garden, apart from the Tree of the Knowledge of Good and Evil, the consequence of which would be death.[17]

However, Eve, being tempted by the serpent, convinced Adam to share in the fruit of the Tree of the Knowledge of Good and Evil. In addition to death, this act of disobedience led to sin in man, which is the natural propensity of man towards violating moral rule.[18] Through disobedience, man's nature was now corrupted and because of these things, Paul could write that we are slaves to sin[19] and that man requires salvation.[20]

But, from what am I being saved? While we certainly need to be saved from a corrupt moral nature and the related offences and consequences, this sin also led to death. We all get to experience death, because sin entered the world through one man, and then death

---

[17] Genesis 2:17
[18] Romans 5:12
[19] Romans 6:17
[20] Romans 1:16

spread to all men, because all sinned.[21] This suggests that sin and death are interdependent problems, which leads us to the possibility that salvation should include a rescue from death; an idea confirmed by Jesus, who said that everyone who believes in him would never die.[22]

To explain this and other issues more clearly, careful note must be given to how the Genesis narrative defines death. This is an important issue, because there are at least two variations of thought on the nature of death. The first is usually based on a combination of ideas, including the belief that man was created with an immortal 'soul', and God's warning to man that he would die in the day that he sinned.[23] Because of these ideas, some believe that the death of man was actually a separation from God, or a type of spiritual death. While the body would die, man's soul would survive, although spiritually alienated from God.

Therefore, the emphasis of this 'death' was the change in the state of the relationship between God and Man. While this *death* also eventually led to a bodily death, it has become more theologically significant, because it is seen as the primary causative act leading to the secondary consequence (the death of the body).

However, an emphasis on this view of death is contradicted by a clearly stated definition in Genesis

---

[21] Romans 5:12
[22] John 11:25
[23] Genesis 2:17

3:19. "By the sweat of your face you shall eat bread, till you return to the ground, because from it you were taken; for you are dust, and to dust you shall return."[24] In fact, God's definition of death was so clearly stated that it seems remarkable that there could be any debate. It is also very important to note that the definition does not mention any other possibility for man after death.

The definition was reinforced by the use of four significant interacting phrases, which are really two pairs of repeated ideas.[25] The double parallelism of thought emphasizes not only the seriousness of the consequences, but also the reality of the outcome for man. The phrase ...*for you are dust,* clearly states that man is only dust and nothing else. The phrase ...*to dust you shall return,* suggests that the death of man under judgment requires the destruction of the body.

Genesis very carefully explained that without the body, man could not continue to exist. However, these ideas are likely to be ignored or misunderstood when the belief is a spiritual death, supported by the observation that man did not immediately die.

While it is true that man was told he would '*die in the day*' that he ate from the Tree of the Knowledge of Good and Evil, this statement was most likely a Hebrew idiom; it meant that the consequence for disobedience would be a definite certainty. An example

---

[24] Genesis 3:19 (NASB)
[25] Genesis 3:19

of this is found in 1 Kings 2:37. In this passage, Solomon put Shimei under house arrest, forbidding him to leave the city under the threat of death, which would occur *on the day* that he attempted to leave. However, Shimei left Jerusalem to seek two escaped slaves in Gath, and it was not until he returned that the king commanded that he be put to death.[26]

Therefore, while Adam and Eve did not experience physical death the very same day they ate from the Tree of the Knowledge of Good and Evil, the fulfilment of the judgment remained an inevitable event. If speeding down the road I am captured by a speed camera, the consequence is certain although I may not receive the fine for some days. Because God clearly defined death as the dissolution of the body, it is reasonable to accept the idiomatic explanation that man became subject to the process of physical death.

The emphasis on the body's eventual destruction is significant, because it demonstrated the mortality of man. Without the body's continued existence, there was no hope for man.

While the consequence of disobedience seemed distinctively focussed on the mortal state of man's condition, there may be no problem in accepting the idea of a broken spiritual relationship when man sinned. His attempt to cover his nakedness suggests an

---

[26]MacDonald, W., & Farstad, A. 1997, c1995. *Believer's Bible Commentary : Old and New Testaments* (1 Ki 2:36). Thomas Nelson: Nashville

altered state of self-awareness and a troubled conscience. Unable to choose to do what is right, sin and rebellion only served to separate man further from the care of God's providence without apparent solution. Disobedience now brought to man the fruit of spiritual death. A downward cycle of spiritual corruption would grow more apparent, leading to hatred and murder. It describes man as utterly lost to life and purpose and without hope.

These ideas led Paul to state that prior to our faith in Christ we were dead in our trespasses and sins.[27] However, this *spiritual death* cannot actually be death *itself,* if God has already defined it as the dissolution of the physical self. The concept that the body decays when it dies created a crucial existential dilemma. This act of decay determined the end of man, creating the need for a meaningful solution.

While Genesis gave us a very clear definition of what death is, it says nothing about what happens after death, a significant point that is often simply overlooked. Because this passage does not define what happens after death, it should lead us to look more closely at death itself. In addition, any conceivable views of man's state of existence after death, need to be explored in the context of its definition.

Death according to God, was the end of self and the dissolution of the body, and there was no indication

---

[27] Ephesians 2:1 (NRSV)

that it was anything else other than this. This does not constitute an argument against the possibility of life after death, but an attempt to avoid making death something it is not, especially when there is a perfectly good definition of what it is.

It is also important to point out that this death does not seem to lead to any future existence, only because nothing was said about any such possibility. Understanding these points will become useful, when investigating what the rest of the Bible does say about life after death.

If God's judgment is physical death, then that suggests that man does not actually exist after he has died. To suggest otherwise would be contradictory to the purpose of the judgment. In this case, there is really only one solution; the hope that God will bring us back to life!

However, the alternative solution requires the incongruous idea that man must somehow naturally survive death. This position assumes different ideas about the nature of death and requires man to be an immortal being who is unable to die. It suggests that at the moment of physical death, man must continue to exist in some other immaterial form, an idea that will become a subject of discussion during this book.

Therefore, the two options have to be carefully understood in the context in which the definition of death was made. In Genesis, there was no apparent solution for death. This means that either man dies and ceases to exist (until God brings him back to life), or man immediately continues to exist in some other form after death. If man was created an immortal being, then the idea of a spiritual separation as being death either in this world or the next, would not only be valid, but essential. However, this thinking leads us away from God's definition of death, which appears to exclude the idea of immortality.

In addition to these issues, the function of the Tree of Life and the Tree of the Knowledge of Good and Evil becomes essential in understanding the problem of death. When the serpent tempted Eve to eat from the Tree of the Knowledge of Good and Evil, she was told that she would not really die.[28] This was a lie to secure the death of man by placing before him the temptation of being God-like. Having chosen from the Tree of the Knowledge of Good and Evil, man now became subject to the curse of death. However, God, concerned that man would now eat from the Tree of Life and live-forever in his fallen state, sent him out of the Garden. In addition, a cherubim and a flaming sword were placed to prevent man's return.[29] The nature of this banishment unequivocally dispossessed man of his right to the Tree of Life.

Because this passage of Scripture clearly stated that man still had the potential to live forever, even in

---

[28] Genesis 3:4
[29] Genesis 3:22-24 (NKJV)

his fallen state, it suggests that the immortality of man was always dependent on access to the Tree of Life. This made his immortality conditional. The condition was obedience to God's law and the Tree of Life was the source of his immortality, which means that man could not have been naturally immortal. Man had no immunity from death once he was expelled from the garden, and the presence of the cherubim and flaming sword made certain the judgment of death.

However, there are potential problems with the idea of man's dependence on a tree of life. The fact that man could have eaten from the Tree of Life and overcome the curse of death, leads us to entertain the thought that the Tree of Life had amazing supernatural powers. Also, consider the fact that God set up the cherubim and a flaming sword to stop man from gaining access to the Tree of Life.[30] What has happened to the cherubim and the flaming sword? Appeal to human reason and thought cannot answer questions like these.

It also becomes problematic to expect a literal interpretation of the text, if that creates further difficulties. For example, theoretically, man might have been subject to death regardless of whether he was obedient or not. For instance, imagine that Adam trips over, knocks himself out, and dies from a nasty bump on the head before eating from either tree.

---

[30] Genesis 3:24

To understand the importance of the message, the purpose needs to be understood. The narrative is answering existential questions. Why do I exist and why do I die? Understanding the message of choice requires us to look beyond our own suppositions, especially in a story that includes an etiological motif that explains how snakes lost their legs. For the literalist view that tends to see Scripture dictated to human authors by God, the creation story, described using mythical language such as a talking snake and special trees, must be by necessity the actual reality.

However, "the view that the Bible is basically dictated is inadequate since it fails to recognise the human dimension of the Bible."[31] While we do not want to become distracted by the debate between historical, symbolic, and existentialist views, there is a need to consider the more unusual elements of the text. While being divinely inspired, the nature of the language suggests that they are the writer's attempts to use human words and experiences, to describe and explain existential issues as he reflects on underlying meanings. Grenz, who describes Bloesch's view (who can see within Adam the actual and the symbolic), notes that, "we need not understand in a literalistic manner the details of the Genesis narrative of creation and fail to note the point of the description."[32]

---

[31] Paul Trebilco, ed, Considering Orthodoxy: Foundations for Faith Today (Colcom Press, Orewa), 98
[32] Grenz, Community of God, 197

Considering these issues, we should not be surprised to see that the use of a tree or plant, was sometimes used as an "image of the life giving power of the deity or the king and it could also represent cosmic order."[33] A link with immortality was also suggested in some sources, such as the Epic of Gilgamesh, where the 'plant of life' is lost to the serpent when Gilgamesh goes into the water to bathe.[34]

It would appear that the Tree of Life explains to us some existential phenomenon through the lens of metaphorical imagery. God created man with the freedom to choose a course of action that would improve his potential for existence. Man chose to disobey God, ate from the Tree of the Knowledge of Good and Evil, and consequently forfeited his right to life.

This choice to disobey could only be made once. Once made, disobedience removed the possibility of immortality from man's grasp. This was illustrated by man's departure from the garden. Obedience on the other hand, required a continuous choice, and the opportunity for obedience could only exist as long as it could manifest itself in an act of choice, as illustrated by

---

[33] Alice Wood, Of Wings and Wheels: A Synthetic Study of the Biblical Cherubim, Volume 385 of Beihefte Zur Zeitschrift fur die alttestamentliche Wissenschaft, (Walter de Gruyter, 2008), 57
[34] Roland Edmund Murphy, The Tree of Life: An Exploration of Biblical Wisdom Literature, (Wm. B. Eerdmans Publishing), 156

the two trees.[35] Therefore, Man had the possibility of immortality dependent on his continued obedience, allowing him to remain in God's presence and enjoy the fruit of immortality. These ideas are reinforced by God's definition of death, which states that the end of man's existence results from disobedience leading to the dissolution of the body.

It is also important to note that the dissolution of the body occurred outside the Garden, and away from God's presence and the Tree of Life. The irony is that the significance of the Tree of Life only becomes apparent to man once he has chosen from the Tree of the Knowledge of Good and Evil.

*". . . Adam only reaches out for the fruit of the tree of life after he has fallen prey to death . . . Adam has eaten of the tree of knowledge, but the thirst for the tree of life, which this fruit has given him, remains unquenched . . . The tree of life is guarded by the power of death; it remains untouchable, divinely unapproachable."*[36]

The severity of the outcome described by the presence of the Cherubim and flaming sword, emphatically declares that all hope for immortality is lost. The way back to God was now fiercely blocked. To

---

[35] The Apostle Paul explains these ideas in Romans 7:7-13. Without the law Paul would not have known sin. However, sin used the law to produce all sorts of covetousness within him. Consequently, the law that had promised him life brought him death.

[36] D. Bonhoeffer, Creation and Fall (London: SCM, 1966) 89-92.

make matters worse, man's thirst for knowledge made him painfully aware of the choice that he should have made. He longs for immortality, but he cannot overcome the flaming sword and Cherubim. If he is to experience immortality, death must now somehow be defeated. Here is man's great dilemma. Who will rescue me from death? Who will save me from the grave?

From this existential crisis, man has formed a myriad of culturally expressed solutions. The Biblical answer is that death has been defeated not by the first Adam, but by a second Adam to "set free all who have lived their lives as slaves to the fear of dying."[37] "He will wipe every tear from their eyes, and there will be no more death or sorrow or crying or pain. All these things are gone forever."[38] In the Book of Revelation, the Tree of Life is once again offered to man, but only those that have washed their robes will be able to enter the gates of the city.[39]

The language mirrors that of the Genesis creation narrative. In both of these references, the Tree of Life is a revelation of the promise that God provides life based on certain conditions. Man, having chosen to ignore those conditions, lost his opportunity for life and found himself subject to the futility of death. However, those that wash their robes are those that have been sanctified and justified. They now find themselves the

---

[37] Hebrews 2:14-15 (NLT)
[38] Revelation 21:4 (NLT)
[39] Revelation 22:14

recipients of the life from which death had previously disqualified their participation.

# The Creation of Man

Whatever views are formed on the initial state of man's nature in the Garden, Scripture states that man faces a clearly defined physical death. There was also no evidence in the creation narrative that would suggest that man naturally continued to exist in any form after this death. Therefore, any possibility for future existence must depend on special intervention, which suggests that the immortality of man is conditional. The opposing idea is that man naturally continues to exist beyond his death, or that he is naturally immortal.

This natural immortality describes the nature of man as a created being, who continues to exist beyond his physical death as an immortal soul. Eventually this soul may be reunited with a body. However, this idea contradicts God's definition of death in Genesis that made no mention or suggestion of any such possible future existence. The definition was important, because it is the context by which passages of Scripture that do describe a future existence for man should be understood.

In general, most Christians have accepted the belief that man was created a naturally immortal being, using ideas derived from passages of Scripture such as that found in Genesis 2:7. In this creation narrative, God breathed the breath of life into man and he became a living soul. This suggested the idea of an immortal element within man not subject to death. The body was doomed to die, but the soul was indestructible and escaped the body at death.

This idea was common to various ancient philosophies such as Greek Platonism.[40] Plato believed that souls came from heaven to the world of matter to reside in humans. However, souls longed for the time when they would be released from their physical selves back to the permanent heavenly realms. Therefore, Plato likened the body to a prison and death as salvation for the soul, which could then escape.

The possibility that the Biblical understanding of the nature of man is related to Greek philosophy creates a conundrum. If this sort of idea is correct, then man must exist as a being that is both mortal and immortal. The soul or the immortal part would continue to live on in some form of existence as a disembodied entity. However, to accept this idea it must be clearly defined and explained by Scripture.

It is important to point out that the existence of man's soul or spirit is not the issue. However, understanding the metaphysical nature of man and its relationship to immortality is essential; the possibility

---

[40] Marvin R Wilson, Our father Abraham: Jewish roots of the Christian faith, (Wm. B. Eerdmans Publishing, 1989), 168

that soul or spirit refers to something, other than what has been commonly accepted, becomes the point of departure. Therefore, accurately defining these words becomes important and needs to take into account the use of the original language words. This is because interpreted meanings, based on common usage, may modify our Biblical Anthropology in ways that are contradictory to the purposes of Scripture.[41] Conversely, a correctly understood use of these words should lead to a more accurate explanation of the nature of man.

In Genesis, the *soul* that appears in some translations is used for the Hebrew word *nephesh*. For example, in Genesis 2:7 the LORD God breathed into man the breath of life, and man became a living *nephesh*. Throughout Scripture, this word *nephesh* was also translated into English by other words such as self, life, person, and heart. It is related to the rare verbal form *napash*, which refers to the essence of life, the act of breathing or taking breath.[42]

While the word *nephesh* was translated *soul* in the King James Bible, in some versions such as the New King James and the New Revised Standard Version, the

---

[41] For example…"The soul, in many mythological, religious, philosophical, and psychological traditions, is the incorporeal and, in many conceptions, immortal essence of a person, living thing, or object." http://en.wikipedia.org/wiki/Soul While there might be a wide variation of belief on the nature of soul, the possibility exists that the general definition obscures or replaces a more accurate Biblical definition.

[42] Vine, W. E., Unger, M. F., & White, W. 1996. Vine's complete expository dictionary of Old and New Testament words (1:237). T. Nelson: Nashville

translators have opted for the word *being*. This is because the word *being* more closely matches the intent of God's creative act that is inherent in the original Hebrew term *nephesh*. God breathed life into man and he became a living *being* or *nephesh*. A being is someone or something that has life in itself. It explains the completeness of the nature of the creature that lives and breathes. There was no indication that the being is immortal or survives death.

In addition to this, *nephesh* is applied not only to men, but also to animals, as in Genesis 1:24 where God says, "Let the earth bring forth living creatures (*nephesh*)."[43] Using the word *soul* as our choice of translation would render the text as, "let the earth bring forth living *souls* of every kind." While the word soul does not sound appropriate in this context, it is important to note that the word *nephesh* described creatures other than man.

If we wish to apply great significance to the fact that man has a soul, then this significance can only be undermined by the idea that animals were also created living souls. If animals have souls, then what does that say about the soul of man? To answer this question, it must be noted that it says that the earth brought forth the living *nephesh* according to its kind. This suggests that the *nephesh* is actually the creature itself.

This is not the only instance when the word was

---

[43] NRSV

used to describe creatures as living beings. In Genesis 1:30 in the New King James Version, the word *life* was translated from *nephesh* and *chay*. *Chay* means alive or living and as seen before, *nephesh* means creature or being. This verse talks about everything that creeps on the earth in which there is life. The nuance of meaning reflects the idea that life and creature are synonymous with the concept of a *nephesh*. The word *nephesh* can also mean '*that which breathes*'. Therefore, the New Revised Standard Version translates these words in Verse 30 as, everything that has the '*breath of life*'.

In Genesis 2:7, another word used similar imagery. *Nashamah*, meaning a puff of wind or angry, vital breath, was used alongside *chay* (alive, living) to form the phrase *breath of life*. This phrase then supports the next phrase in the same verse where it says that man became a living being (*chay nephesh*). The idea here is that only God can give life to inanimate clay. He breathed into man the breath of life and made him a living being.

There is no indication that the process of creation involved a separate and immortal soul within man. The use of these words helps to explain, that the act of creation involved making inanimate objects alive through the breath of life. God breathed life into man, man became a living creature, and this imagery was used for all the animals.

Because the act of breathing was the indispensable proof that a being has life, and the soul appeared to be the creature itself, then it is unlikely that Scripture meant something different. The idea that a 'soul' could separate from the body or survive death, would be contradictory to the description of a living, breathing and autonomous creature, who was made from organic materials. The use of the word soul in the rest of Scripture will be discussed in a later chapter.

In addition to the idea of the soul, the creation narrative stated that man was made in the *image* and *likeness* of God.[44] While the idea that the gods made creatures out of clay and breathed life into them is found in various mythologies,[45] the use of *image* and *likeness* suggests a unique relationship between God and his creation. The word image (*tselem*) meant a statue, image, or copy and could describe such things as idols or figures that one made to represent a god. It could also be used to describe the role of an object or person, who would represent the purpose and authority of another. "The kings of the ancient Near East often left images of themselves in those cities or territories where they could not be present in person. Such images served to represent their majesty and power."[46]

Other uses of image also help to capture the nuance of thought. For example, in Psalm 39:6, *tselem* means a "shadow" of a thing, which means that the

---

[44] Gen 1:26
[45] http://en.wikipedia.org/wiki/Creation_of_man_from_clay
[46] Grenz, Community of God, 174

original is not represented precisely and that the thing lacks its essential characteristic or reality.[47] The word likeness comes from *demut*, meaning a pattern whose specifications are used in making a copy. These ideas suggest that the word "image" attributes particular essential qualities to the object, which is being patterned after the original.

While it might be suggested that this 'image' incorporates a metaphysical and immortal element, such an idea is probably dependent on the understanding that God gave man a 'soul'. In other words, the assumption has to be made that because God is an immortal Spirit, God gives man an immortal soul, and therefore man is made of spiritual 'stuff'. However, as we have already seen, the soul seems to be the life that God gives in creation through the breath of life. It would also seem pointless postulating an explanation that this element exists and is unaffected by death, because this contradicts an already clearly defined antithesis.

There is also another problem over the possibility that man's construction included a separable immortal being. When God created man, he gave him the ability to reproduce after his own kind. In addition, Scripture tells us that Adam was able to beget a son in his own likeness and after his image.[48] The

---

[47] Vine, W. E., Unger, M. F., & White, W. 1996.
[48] Genesis 5:3 (NASB)

origin of a 'soul'[49] for Seth then becomes problematic, because while Adam and Eve had the ability to procreate physically, there was no suggestion that this involved the creation of an immortal element.

While King David acknowledged that it was the Lord that formed his inward parts, there was no sense that he was speaking of a part of his being that was separate from his physical self. It was more likely to be his acknowledgment of the miracle of life. "You made all the delicate, inner parts of my body and knit me together in my mother's womb."[50] The word knit described the complex way in which the body was constructed as interwoven connections of flesh and bone. While the formation of the fetus was an act of genetically organized processes, it was God who had ordained the process.

Therefore, if Seth were to have a 'soul', God would have been required to supernaturally implant this 'soul' at the moment of conception.[51] However, the idea that God implanted an immortal being into the fertilized egg is illogical, considering that Scripture explained that Adam begat a son in his own likeness and after his own image. This issue was a recognized

---

[49] As stated elsewhere, these elements may exist as a part of man and we do not deny their existence. But, it is important to note the distinction between the mortal nature of man and the possibility of naturally immortal supernaturally included aspects of his construction.

[50] Psalm 139:13 (NLT)

[51] The suggestion that God creates this part of man is based on ideas already discussed from Gen 2:7 that God breathes living 'souls' into man.

problem throughout Christian history and it produced a variety of theories. For example, Lactantius, Thomas Aquinas and Peter Lombard saw souls created by God ex nihilo at the moment of their infusion into the body, while Origen saw souls as pre-existent. These beliefs make assumptions that are not stated in Scripture and therefore, when it says that Adam begat a son in his own image, it is very likely that Seth's construction was the product of the genetic make-up of his parents.

The problems created by these ideas lead some evangelical scholars to note that, "while man is made in God's image, immortality is no more an essential quality of God than omnipotence and omniscience, yet no one has considered these to be inherent in the creature man."[52]

Consideration could be given to the possibility that an 'immortal image' was lost in the fall. However, conjecture over the nature of man in the Garden tends to overshadow the central themes of the story. The real point was that man could not keep the law, and consequently became subject to the law's penalty. This caused man to become aware of the need for immortality, which he could not obtain by his own efforts.

Being made in God's image is important, because it makes human beings unique and

---

[52] Edward William Fudge, The Fire That Consumes (Houston: Providential Press, 1982), 59

differentiates them from the animal kingdom. We could say that man's ability to function in abstract, relational, and sacred activities suggests a moral, spiritual, and intellectual capacity that may be indicative of those special qualities that were imprinted on him in creation. However, it is apparent from Scripture that sin has destroyed the quality of this image, as evident by the way in which humankind has failed to fulfil God's laws. "None is righteous, no, not one; no one understands; no one seeks for God. All have turned aside; together they have become worthless; no one does good, not even one."[53]

In the New Testament, the solution and expectation was that man would put on the new self, so that he might be renewed in the image of Christ. This renewal was initially a process leading to a sanctified nature, and then finally a transformation into the image of the heavenly man in the resurrection.[54]

Whatever the views on what the image of God might be, and whether it was lost in the fall of man, there was no obvious indication that it was an immortal soul. The emphasis of Scripture was on explaining man's creation as a living breathing creature, whose disobedience led to death. This death did not seem to be anything else other than the dissolution of the body, as it returned to the basic components from which it

---

[53] Romans 3:10-12 (ESV)
[54] Romans 8:29, 1 Corinthians 15:49, 2 Corinthians 3:18, Colossians 3:10,

was constructed. This idea is contrary to the possibility that man is a supernatural being capable of defeating death.

# *Soul*

In our attempts to understand the potential for man's future existence, we have briefly touched on Plato's ideas about the immortality of the soul, and the possible influence this has had on Christian thinking. If these beliefs were Biblical, then we would expect to see scriptural evidence supporting the idea of an immortal soul.

## *Soul in the Old Testament*

While there are over 400 occurrences where the Hebrew word *nephesh* was translated as soul, there was actually no equivalent in the Hebrew language to describe the nature of man suggested by *soul*, as defined in general use. The concept of the immortal soul was Greek in origin and unknown in Hebrew thought, which understood man to have an inner self and an outer appearance. The outer appearance was *shem*, which was most commonly translated name and defined a person's reputation. The inner self was *nephesh*,[55] defined in the creation story as the clay form

---

[55] Vine, W. E., Unger, M. F., & White, W. 1996.

brought to life by the breath of God.

The metaphorical portrayal of man animated by the 'breath of life' suggested that he *was* a living soul, as opposed to something that *has* a soul. There was no indication that this soul was immortal or separable from man himself, and the emphasis was on the person as a complete unit. These ideas support the observation that, "Theological anthropology now generally focuses on a unitary view of humanity... It affirms that the whole person is made in God's image and views the immortality of the soul as quite possibly an alien Greek intrusion."[56]

The way in which *nephesh* was used elsewhere supports the Hebrew view of man as a complete being. For example, *nephesh* could also be translated as life or self, as in Leviticus 17:11, which says that the life (*nephesh*) of the flesh is in the blood. If this verse were translated, "The soul of the flesh is in the blood," it would not sound correct, especially in the context of Greek origins and extra Biblical usage. However, when the word is translated life, it not only makes sense, but also corresponds with its use in the creation narrative. A creature is a being that has life - the creature has *nephesh*.

Because context dictates that *nephesh* should be translated as life, it also tells us something about the

---

[56] Kurian, G. T. (2001). *Nelson's new Christian dictionary : The authoritative resource on the Christian world.* Nashville, Tenn.: Thomas Nelson Pubs.

nuance of meaning that can be attributed to its use. In this verse, it makes significant sense, because without blood, the flesh cannot survive and will die, and therefore even the King James Version translates *nephesh* as life rather than soul. The important idea here is that the *nephesh* is dependent on the functions of the body. The connection between the act of breathing, circulation and the life of the *nephesh* suggests that man was thought of as an organic being, who could not exist without these important physiological functions. This suggests that the soul remains dependent on the body for its continued survival.

The idea that the soul was actually the individual was also brought out in the use of parallelism in Hebrew, which served to reinforce and explain ideas. An example of this can be found in Psalm 3:2, which says, "Many are saying of my *soul*, there is no deliverance for *him* in God."[57] In the first part of the verse, the word soul is *nephesh*, and in the second part, the parallel counterpart is the personal pronoun *him*. The soul is the person who is spoken of as having no deliverance in God. This nuance is picked up by the New American Bible, which uses *me* instead of soul. This could be paraphrased, "they tell me that there is no deliverance for me." *Him* and *soul* are synonymous. This type of scriptural emphasis indicates that the soul was considered to be the person.

---

[57] Psalm 3:2 (NASB)

*Nephesh* was also used as the parallel for the Lord. An example of this is found in Psalm 11:5, which says that the Lord tests the righteous, but his soul hates the one who loves violence. In the second part of this poetic parallelism, the word soul *(nephesh)* was used as the synonymous replacement word. Here the word *nephesh* was not talking about a separate and divisible being, but was used as an equivalent term for the primary speaker, who in this case is God himself. Therefore this verse says that the Lord tests the righteous, but the wicked, the one who loves violence, He himself (with all his being) hates. In this case, *nephesh* does not seem to describe the nature of metaphysical matter, but is used to refer to the person.

The idea that *nephesh* can often simply mean a person is found elsewhere. For instance, in Ezekiel 18:4 it says that the soul who sins would die. It could be suggested that this soul is an immortal element that brings death to the body because of sin. However, the idea that the word *nephesh* in this context does not simply apply to a living person, is contradicted by other passages, which emphasise this particular nuance. For example, in Numbers 35:15, it says that if anyone kills a *nephesh* they can flee to a refuge city. The important point here is that the *nephesh* was thought of as the person whose life could be terminated.

Therefore, the person could also be subject to capital punishment as in Exodus 31:14, where it says that any person that worked on the Sabbath would be put to death…that *soul* would be cut off from among his people. In this passage, Hebrew parallelism combines death with the *soul* being cut off. There was no sense that the soul who was cut off continued to exist as an immortal being, because the emphasis of Scripture was on the consequence, which was death.

While God says that all *souls* are his, it is important to emphasise that he also says in the same verse that the *soul* who sins will die.[58] This could be rephrased; all belong to him, but the 'person' who sins will die. Life is a blessing from God and sin leads to the loss of this life. The emphasis was always on the value of life and avoiding death.

Therefore, the person enjoyed life and death resulted in the loss of *nephesh*, as described in the death of Rachel.[59] Although the text states that her *soul* left her as she lay dying, this does not suggest an immortal 'Rachel' escaping death. Considering the context in which *nephesh* was used to describe the creature animated by the breath of life, the loss of *nephesh* becomes synonymous with death, the end of the creature and the end of life itself. It was an idiomatic description of the end of personhood, which is evident by the loss of all those things that one associates with a living being. Therefore, Rachel's death "does not indicate that the soul was considered a separate entity

---

[58] Ezekiel 18:4 (ESV)
[59] Genesis 35:18

from the body with an existence of its own, but only that the life was departing."[60] This idea was also reinforced by the fact that the verse included the phrase, "for she was dying." There seemed to be no interest in the possible future state of Rachel's soul, because her death was understood to be the end of her life.

In general, there does not seem to be any precise details in the Old Testament about what happened to a person or soul after they died. While in death the soul seemed destined for the grave,[61] the word usually stood for a living person who was alive. Death was seen as the archenemy of the soul. It required a rescue[62] from death, which suggests that death was the end of the soul. For example, the Psalmist could say, "You brought my soul up from the grave; you have kept me alive, that I should not go down to the pit."[63]

The idea that the *nephesh* was a being in this life that abhorred the thought of death in the grave, was brought out in many other scriptures. The Psalmist complained; "What will you gain if I die, if I sink into the grave? Can my dust praise you? Can it tell of your faithfulness?"[64] Likewise, Job's hope was that his soul

---

[60] Radmacher, E. D., Allen, R. B., & House, H. W. 1999. Nelson's new illustrated Bible commentary (Ge 35:18). T. Nelson Publishers: Nashville
[61] The destination of the 'soul' in the Old Testament is also discussed in a later chapter.
[62] Psalm 33:18-19 (NRSV)
[63] Psalm 30:3 (NKJV)
[64] Psalm 30:9 (NLT)

would be redeemed from the pit (the grave). It was the desire to avoid suffering and death, and the expectation of a return to 'life' that weighed heavily on the mind of Job.[65]

While the loss of life was synonymous with the soul being taken by God,[66] the understanding was that body and soul could be destroyed in death. For example, Isaiah says that the Lord will destroy both soul and body, and in true Hebrew style provides the parallelism to help explain the meaning...It will be as when a sick man wastes away.[67] Therefore, the Hebrew emphasis was about avoiding death or returning from a place of death or near death and enjoying life. Death was the antithesis of life.

These ideas are exemplified throughout the Psalms where *nephesh* can simply be translated as life. For example, David could say, "Lord, I lift up my life....keep my life and deliver me....gather not my life with sinners....you have brought up my life from the grave."[68]

While the avoidance of death was important, the *nephesh* also longed for a quality of life. When Balaam was called to curse Israel, he ended up offering a blessing instead. "Who can count the dust of Jacob, or number the dust-cloud of Israel? Let me (*my nephesh*)

---

[65] Job 33:28
[66] Job 27:8
[67] Isaiah 10:18 (ESV)
[68] Psalm 25:1,20 Psalm 26:9, Psalm 30:3 (ESV) Paraphrased

die the death of the upright, and let my end be like his!"[69] Here *nephesh* becomes the idiom for self and it is used of "man as being mortal, subject to death of various kinds, from which it can be saved and delivered and life prolonged."[70] Balaam hoped that the nature of his death, which he understood to be the end of his *nephesh*, would be like the end of the righteous whom he knew were blessed.[71]

The idea that one could hope for an improvement in the quality of life was exemplified in the marriage of Ruth to Boaz. The petition of Naomi proffered Boaz as a restorer of life (*nephesh*), and subsequently, after the hardship of being poor and widowed, Ruth's quality of life would improve.[72] *Nephesh* was also used to describe romantic attachment as in Genesis 34:3, where Shechem's soul was drawn to Dinah because he loved her. The use of soul to idiomatically express relationship was also exemplified by Jonathan and David, whose souls were knit together.[73]

These types of expressions are found elsewhere in Scripture. For example, in Genesis 42:21, Joseph's brothers acknowledged the distress that they had brought to the *soul* of their brother. There is no

---

[69] Numbers 23:10 (NRSV)
[70] Smith, J. H. (1992; Published in electronic form, 1996). The new treasury of scripture knowledge : Nashville TN: Thomas Nelson.
[71] Numbers 22:12
[72] Ruth 4:15
[73] 1 Samuel 18:1 (ESV)

indication that the use of the word described an immortal element of Joseph. Rather, it was the life of Joseph that suffered because of the actions of his brothers. In 1 Samuel 1:15, Hannah poured out her soul before the Lord. This is an idiomatic statement that explains the intensity of feeling in Hannah's petition to the Lord. In 1 Samuel 30:6, the people were 'bitter' in soul, because David's men had lost their wives and children, who had been captured by the Amalekites.

It needs to be remembered that in these sorts of examples we could simply use the word life. For example, Hannah poured out her life before the Lord, Jonathan and David's lives were knit together, and Schechem's life was drawn to Dinah. Understanding how language functions to communicate ideas is essential in interpreting Scripture. Understanding the nature of man, as explained by the Old Testament, requires us to consider the overall emphasis. In this case, it seems that the *soul* referred to the person or the life of the person.

It is also important to point out what Scripture does not emphasise. There does not appear to be any clear or consistent pattern of teaching, which might suggest that the *soul* exists separably from man as an immortal element that naturally survives death. If that idea were true, we would expect to see passages of Scripture that described the *soul* passing on into an afterlife experience, leaving the body and the care and concerns of the world behind.

This last point is significant, because it was life in the body that seemed to be the source of man's afflictions, and yet he still seemed to hope for a quality of life that was experienced in bodily form. There was no 'escapism' like that defined by Greek philosophical expectations, where the *soul* longed to be free of the body.

### *Soul in the New Testament*

In the New Testament, the word "soul" is sometimes used to translate the Greek word *psuche*. However, *psuche* is also translated by other words as well. For example, it is translated about forty times[74] in the New Testament as 'life' or 'lives'. Jesus says that we are not to worry about our life, which suggests the present life experienced in bodily form.[75]

Therefore, understanding the way in which such words are translated has important implications. Sometimes the same Greek word is translated by different English words. Sometimes the same English word is used to translate different Greek words in different contexts. Sometimes an English word remains, even though it could be replaced by a more

---

[74] Enhanced Strong's Lexicon, 1995, (Woodside Bible Fellowship -Electronic version)
[75] Matthew 6:25

effective equivalent. The task of the translator is to find a word that matches the intent of the writer, by taking into consideration the context in which that word is found.

The use of *psuche* is no exception. Not only is it translated in many different ways, it is also used in a variety of contexts. For example, 1 Peter 3:20 says that eight souls were saved in Noah's ark[76] and Acts 7:14 says that Joseph sent and called his father Jacob, and all his relatives to him, seventy-five people (Souls).[77] In these contexts, a person is someone who was living. Obviously different translations have sought to clarify the meaning, by choosing the best word to bring out the original intent of the writer. However, in the above examples, the New King James Version has used different English words for the same Greek word, even though it was used in similar contexts.

Considering these ideas, it becomes difficult and unreasonable to use one single English word, to define or defend the concept of an immortal soul. For example, in 2 Corinthians 12:15 in the New King James Version, the word *souls* could be *lives*, but the New Revised Standard Version simply used the word *you*. The use of personal pronouns for *psuche* is also exemplified in Mark 14:34, where Jesus says, "I am deeply grieved."[78] The New King James version translates this as, "My

---

[76] 1 Peter 3:20 (NKJV)
[77] Acts 7:14 (NKJV)
[78] Mark 14:34 (NRSV)

soul is exceedingly sorrowful."[79] In Matthew 12:18, the subject was the Lord speaking through the prophet Isaiah, whose soul was well pleased.

The word is also used in many other ways. In Luke 2:35 it says that a sword will pierce Mary's soul, which describes the emotional pain in observing her son's death. In Acts 14:2, the unbelieving Jews stirred up the Gentiles and poisoned their minds (*psuche*) against the brethren. In Philippians 1:27, Paul urged his readers to stand fast in one spirit, with one mind (*psuche*) for the faith of the gospel. In Ephesians 6:6, we are told to do the will of God, not as men-pleasers, but as from the heart (*psuche*). Scripture also tells us that souls can be purified by obeying the truth,[80] strengthened by ministry,[81] and they have hope as an anchor.[82] In Acts 27:22, it says that there would be no loss of life (*psuche*), even though the ship was in danger of sinking. The soul in this case was a person who could die by drowning.

All of these uses of the word *psuche* are very similar to that found in the Old Testament. Like *nephesh*, *psuche* was the multipurpose vernacular used to describe those things where the English language uses life, person, mind, heart, and self.

While there are scriptures that might seem to

---

[79] Mark 14:34 (NKJV)
[80] 1 Peter 1:22
[81] Acts 14:22
[82] Hebrews 6:19

suggest that the soul is more than just the person, interpretive solutions require us to consider the context of these scriptures, while taking into account an understanding of the use of the word in other passages. For example, the apostle John sees in a vision, "the souls of all who had been martyred for the word of God, and for being faithful in their testimony."[83] The first thing to note is that this is an event that John records while he is in the spirit, and is a vision of things that are yet to happen. Because Jesus said that they were "things that must soon take place,"[84] they were a preview of real world events, symbolically describing those things that were about to occur to those to whom the message was given.[85]

Secondly, the idea of one's voice crying out after death is an idiomatic expression of injustice. This was exemplified in the murder of Abel, where the voice of his blood cried out from the ground.[86] Therefore, the souls of the martyrs are like the blood of sacrificial animals poured out at the foot of the altar. They cry out for the avenging of their blood upon those who dwell on the earth. This suggests that their persecutors were still alive on earth at the time John saw the vision, which confirms the idea that this passage symbolically

---

[83] Revelation 6:9 (NLT)
[84] Revelation 1:1 ESV
[85] However, the last few chapters appear to refer to end time events.
[86] Genesis 4:10

describes real world events.[87]

Thirdly, these souls were told to rest a little longer, until the number of their fellow servants, brothers and sisters were killed, as they themselves had been killed,[88] which suggests that they are actually dead. However, in John's vision, these souls are people who seem to be alive. Therefore, the imagery is clearly symbolic. Even though they were dead, like Abel they were still able to 'speak'.[89]

Lastly, there was no evidence of the resurrection or judgment in these passages. According to Hebrews, it was appointed for man to die once, and after that came the judgment,[90] while Paul expected the resurrection to be an end time event, when those who were dead were caught up with those who were still alive.[91] In addition, the Final Judgment takes place towards the end of Revelation after the resurrection - where it seems that parts of the final chapters refer to events that occur after the completion of the real world events. These ideas do not suggest an intermediate state of existence, with souls 'waiting' between death and judgment.

By connecting all of these points, we can suggest that the meaning of the text is more symbolic than

---

[87] Gregg, S. (1997). *Revelation, four views: A parallel commentary* (Re 6:9-11). Nashville, Tenn.: T. Nelson Publishers.
[88] Revelation 6:11
[89] Hebrews 11:4
[90] Hebrews 9:27 (ESV)
[91] 1 Thessalonians 4:17

literal. It was not intended to describe exact metaphysical realities, but to give hope to the persecuted.

Therefore, it is possible that some of these passages in Revelation, refer to actual events during the early persecution of Christians, and possibly also during the destruction of the temple in AD 70. This idea is supported by Jesus' condemnation of Jerusalem when he predicted: "that upon you may come all the righteous blood shed on earth, from the blood of righteous Abel to the blood of Zechariah...whom you murdered between the sanctuary and the altar...all this will come upon this generation."[92] "Therefore the destruction of Jerusalem in that generation was the sentence of the divine Judge in response to the cries of the blood (souls) of the righteous ones slain by her leaders." [93]

Regardless of whether we accept these ideas, there is no indication that using the word soul forces us to interpret it as an immortal component of man that survives death. In this context, *psuche* could still also be translated as people and even lives. This latter point is important in understanding how preconceptions influence the way we interpret Scripture. There is a big difference between the 'soul' that we imagine from Greek philosophy, and the 'soul' that symbolically

---

[92] Matthew 23:35-36 (NRSV)
[93] Gregg, S. (1997).

describes the life of a person.

For example, Jesus said that the man who loves his life (*psuche*) would lose it, while the man who hates his life in this world will keep it for eternal life (*zoe*).[94] These two different types of *life* are essential for understanding the nature of man and the possibility for future existence. Jesus contrasts the pursuit of self-interest for one's own life as opposed to the life that God grants. Jesus was about to surrender his *psuche* life in death, a selfless act by which God was able to offer every believer a quality of life that goes far beyond whatever this life can offer. There is no indication that the life or soul that one surrenders to the purposes of God, is anything other than the whole self. This idea was exemplified in the crucifixion of Christ. For example, in Matthew 20:28, Jesus says that the Son of man came to give his life (*psuche*) as a ransom for the many.

While Scripture sometimes seems to differentiate the soul from the body, this does not necessarily mean that the soul is a divisible and immortal component. For example, in Matthew 10:28 it says that we should not fear those who can kill the body, but cannot kill the soul. However, if we consider the second part of the verse, it says that we should fear him who can destroy both body and soul in hell

---

[94] John 12:25

(*gehenna*).[95] The point is that God can destroy both body and soul together. The soul does not appear to be immortal or indestructible because it survives only as long as the body does.

The fact that it says that God can destroy both body and soul together, and that this is a far greater fate, suggests a judgment process that makes provision for the possibility of either life or death after the body has died. However, the soul still requires a body because they are both destroyed together. While man may kill the body, which is the outward appearance, only God can resurrect, judge and destroy the inner self along with the body. This fate is far worse than what man can do to just the body.

This idea is supported by the reference to *gehenna*. Jesus referred to a well-known physical location near Jerusalem, which had great historical and symbolic significance, and described the final destination of those that were destroyed. "Long before the time of Jesus, the Valley of Hinnom had become crusted over with connotations of whatever is condemned, useless, corrupt, and forever discarded."[96]

To the Hebrews, Jesus' warning would make perfect sense, because the hope was that the self, complete with body, would be resurrected in the last day. For example, Isaiah says, "Your dead shall live,

---

[95] This word is poorly translated by the English word Hell for which other connotations exist. It will be discussed in more detail further on.
[96] Fudge, The Fire That Consumes, 160

their corpses shall rise. O dwellers in the dust, awake and sing for joy!"[97] The destruction of the *psuche* in *gehenna* would indicate a judgment leaving Israel or self without any future hope. While this passage does suggest the survival of the soul, it cannot be as an immortal and separable element. This is because the soul must remain the whole self that is a function of the physiological processes of the body, because they are both destroyed together. The possibility of the destruction of the body and soul (or the person) is a recurrent theme of Scripture to which we will return to in a later chapter.

The different ways in which *psuche* was used in the New Testament makes it difficult to compare its nature to that described by Greek Philosophy. Unlike the Greek emphasis on escaping the body, the soul seems to have been used to describe a person, the life of a person or an element of person that can be best explained in terms of the function of the body or mind.

---

[97] Isaiah 26:19 (NRSV)

# *Spirit*

The nature of the relationship between the body and the soul, does not appear to suggest the idea that man possesses an immortal component that survives death. Body and soul could be destroyed together, and there was no sense that Jesus expected this destruction to result in some future continuous existence.

To complicate matters further, Scripture also used *spirit* to define aspects of man's nature. The nature of the relationship between body, soul and spirit then raises the possibility of a tripartite being, although such an idea should be clearly defined by Scripture. The etymology of such words also plays a significant role in understanding how these words might be used and understood. For example, *spirit* comes from the Latin *spiritus* meaning breath.[98] However, these words might also be used metaphorically and metaphysically, ideas essential in recognising possible influences on translation and interpretation.

## *Spirit in the Old Testament*

In Ecclesiastes 12:7, it says that the spirit will

---

[98] The word *soul* translates the Greek *psuche*, which is based on the verb *psucho*, meaning to breathe or to blow.

return to God who gave it. This seems to indicate that man has a separable and obviously immortal element unaffected by death. However, the problem with the word spirit is that it has many different nuances and contexts in which it is used, and ways in which it can be understood. In particular, the word spirit in Hebrew (*ruach*) is interchangeable with such words as air, wind, breeze, spirit, Spirit, temper, and courage.[99] For example in Genesis 8:1, it says that God made a wind (*ruach*) to pass over the earth and in Genesis 1:2, it says that the Spirit (*ruach*) of God was hovering over the face of the waters.

However, these words are more than just equivalent choices for translation. In Hebrew, *ruach* is wind or spirit. For instance, the Queen of Sheba was so overwhelmed by Solomon's wealth that she lost her breath; there was no more breath in her; she was breathless; or there was no more spirit in her.[100] The interchangeable nature of the word that was used for both the Spirit of God and an earthly wind, is likely to have significant impact on our understanding of translation and interpretation. For example, Ecclesiastes 12:7 could simply have meant that the *breath* will return to God who gave it.

In the Old Testament, God breathed into man the breath of life. The word breath in the phrase "the

---

[99] Vine, W. E., Unger, M. F., & White, W. 1996.
[100] 1 Kings 10:4-5

breath of life"[101] was *nashamah,* which could mean a puff of wind or angry or vital breath. In context, the likely meaning was that God gave man the puff of vital life giving breath.

While *nashamah* was occasionally translated by spirit, its use in these contexts seemed to describe either man's conscience or his motive.[102] Therefore, the use of spirit does not imply that the writer intended the reader to imagine a divisible and immortal being. The word was more commonly used to describe the breath of man. For example, Job could say that as long as he had breath (*nashamah*) in himself, and the breath (*ruach*) of God in his nostrils, he would not speak wickedness.[103]

The use of synonymous parallelism between *nashamah* (puff of wind) and *ruach* (spirit or wind or breath), suggests the metaphorical explanation of the invisible essence of life and its relationship to its creator. God was seen as the "God of the spirits of all flesh,"[104] because God provided the breath of life and death then came to be seen as the release of the spirit or breath.

This idea was exemplified in Genesis 7:22, which described the death of all those who lived on dry land, and in "whose nostrils was the *breath of the spirit of life.*"[105] This passage also combined *nashamah* with *ruach*

---

[101] Genesis 2:7
[102] Job 26:4, Proverbs 20:27
[103] Job 27:3 (NKJV)
[104] Numbers 27:16 (NASB)
[105] Genesis 7:22 (NKJV)

alongside *chay*, and applied to all life, including all the animals that were destroyed in the flood. The use of *ruach* and *nashamah*, as meaning either spirit or breath, is important in our understanding of the link between physical realities and metaphorical ideas.

The idea that the departure of the spirit or breath is the end of life, is further exemplified by Psalm 146:4, where many translations use breath for *ruach*. While some versions might prefer to use *spirit*, context determines that breath is what is meant. "When their breathing stops, they return to the earth, and in a moment all their plans come to an end."[106]

These ideas are exemplified in another Psalm, which says; "when you take away their breath (*ruach*), they die and return to their dust...When you send forth your Spirit (*ruach*), they are created."[107] While the word *ruach* can mean both wind and spirit, most translators tend to use breath in verse 29 for man, and Spirit for God in verse 30. The New American Bible uses breath for both. Therefore, the breath of God is active in the work of creation and the loss of man's breath is synonymous with his death.

The interchangeable use of breath and spirit, makes it difficult to attempt an argument in support of the idea that *ruach* or *nashamah* can mean a spirit that is immortal and divisible. The spirit, described

---

[106] Psalm 146:4 (NLT)
[107] Psalm 104:29-30 (NRSV)

metaphorically by the use of breath, might possibly suggest something that is more than just intangible elements of a living being. However, the link between the metaphor and the reality is often too close to discern a pattern of specific teaching, which reinforces the idea of a separate spirit being. In other words, the idea that God gives man his spirit is too closely linked with the idea of breath.

It must be remembered that the issue of interchangeable terms usually only arises for the translator, and is not always obvious to the reader. The original language words translated by our *spirit* meant *breath* or *wind*. If the Old Testament writers wanted us to have a more ethereal understanding of the nature of man, they could have used other words such as *owb*. This word occurred about 19 times, and was mostly translated as *familiar spirit*. It was used in the context of witchcraft and necromancy, but never to describe the nature of man.

*Ruach* could also be used to express a variety of other ideas as well. For example, in Proverbs 16:2 it says, "All the ways of a man are pure in his own eyes; but the Lord weighs the spirits."[108] The use of poetic parallelism suggests that in this context, the word appears to mean something like *motives*, which is how the New American Standard Bible translates it.

Job could say that his life was like the wind

---

[108] Proverbs 16:2 (NKJV)

(*ruach*),[109] which suggests purposelessness or emptiness, and the same idea could be attached to 'windy words'.[110] The fact that the phrase 'windy words' in Job 16:3 is translated 'vain words' in the King James Version, and yet is *ruach* in Hebrew, should have significant impact on our understanding of the role of context in interpretation.

Ezekiel 13:3 says that people who follow their own *ruach* have seen nothing, which suggests the meaning of one's mind or one's thinking. In Joshua 2:11, *ruach* refers to courage and in Ecclesiastes 10:4, the word *spirit* could be replaced by the equivalent temper. In Psalm 51:12, it says, "Restore to me the joy of your salvation, and uphold me with a willing spirit."[111] In this verse, David asked for a willing attitude to serve God.

Isaiah places *nephesh* (soul) and *ruach* (breath or spirit) in synonymous parallelism in Isaiah 26:9, which says, "With my *soul* I have desired you...by my *spirit* within me."[112] Here the word *nephesh*, which is synonymous with the idea of the whole person, is made synonymous with the *spirit* within. From these passages, the spirit could be defined as that part of the *nephesh* that functions to express attributes of man's relationship with God. Isaiah may have also meant;

---

[109] Job 7:7
[110] Job 16:3 (NRSV)
[111] Psalm 51:12 (ESV)
[112] NKJV

with my life I have desired you, by my breath within me. Either way, the use of poetic parallelism, which was used to avoid repeating particular words, suggests a close connection or relationship between soul and spirit. For example, Job also used this pattern...*I will speak in the anguish of my spirit; I will complain in the bitterness of my soul.*[113]

Therefore, Proverbs 20:27 could say, "The spirit of man is the lamp of the Lord, searching all the innermost parts of his being."[114] This could suggest that the spirit is also that part of man that is the God conscious part of self, but there is no indication that the spirit exists separably from the person. In addition, these ideas do not suggest an immortal spirit, because the spirit seems to function as an element of self, whose end is a bodily death. The emphasis of Scripture was on expressing the nature of man, and his relationship between life, death and his creator, and not on explaining the metaphysical details of an immortal being.

Insisting on the idea of an immortal spirit might also provide support to the possibility of an immortal soul, which is only likely to create additional problems. For example, the idea that a person was a body, an immortal soul, an immortal spirit and a self would seem theologically dubious. There are also physiological problems if we assume that a

---

[113] Job 7:11 (NRSV)
[114] Proverbs 20:27 (NASB)

disembodied entity separates at death from the body.

While it might be possible to compromise, by explaining that the spirit and soul are in fact immortal, but not separate from self, this would contradict Scripture's teaching that sin leads to death. In other words, man could not be immortal and mortal at the same time. Importantly, the idea of 'immortal man' contradicts Scripture's teaching on sin, death and the bodily resurrection of the dead, which is also the subject of a later chapter.

These problems only exist if we are insistent on the idea that man's construction is more than just organic material. Man was made from dust. Dust is indicative of the essential elements and compounds that contribute to the biological activity that defines us as living, breathing creatures. However, being organic does not prevent us from being 'spiritual'. Because of these issues, it is more probable that the idiomatic use of language uses certain terms to help explain the nature of man and his relationship with God. The use of wind and the intangible nature of its essence to describe facets of the human self cannot be ignored.

### Spirit in the New Testament

Of course, *ruach* is often used to describe God himself, and it is also used of the angels and demons.

The metaphorical language pictures presented by the use of *ruach*, are useful in describing the intangible unseen nature of God. Therefore, we should not be surprised to see that in the New Testament, the word spirit comes from *pneuma,* and also means wind, breath, and spirit.[115]

For example, in Luke 8:55, Jesus restored the life of a little girl and at the very moment that she was revived, it says that her spirit returned. Here the word spirit can be translated by other equivalent terms, such as breath, as in the New American Bible. The New Living Translation says, "At that moment her life returned." This understanding of the connection between breathing and life is similar to that in the Genesis narrative. James used this idea to help explain that a person is justified by works and not by faith alone.[116] When he said, "The body without the spirit is dead,"[117] James did not mean that a body had a separate immortal spirit, and that the body died or is dead without this spirit. He meant, "As a breathless body emits no indication of life, so fruitless faith exhibits nothing more than hypocrisy."[118]

As with *ruach, pneuma* could also be used to describe those intangible elements of human self that

---

[115] Vine, W. E., Unger, M. F., & White, W. 1996.
[116] James 2:24 (NRSV)
[117] James 2:26 (NKJV)
[118] KJV Bible commentary. 1997, c1994 (2591). Thomas Nelson: Nashville

characterize the way we think and feel.[119] Therefore, the way that *pneuma* is understood will be influenced by context and intended meanings. For example, while Mary might have said that her spirit rejoiced in God her saviour, she could also have said, "my heart has rejoiced."[120]

In 1 Thessalonians 5:23, Paul made a benediction in which he spoke of "body, soul, and spirit" being preserved blameless at the coming of the Lord. The focus was not on the construction of man as a tripartite being, with distinctive and divisible elements. It was to emphasise the fact that only God can sanctify the whole person. It is important to note that the original language meaning needs to be taken into account in these verses. Spirit could mean breath, and soul could mean self or person, but also possibly heart or mind. These sorts of statements are idiomatic ways of expressing the complete self. They do not reinforce the thought that man is divisible, but rather that he is thought of as a complete being.

However, there are those scriptures that might possibly argue otherwise, as in Hebrews 12:23, where it speaks of the spirits of just men made perfect. The writer in this case was speaking of the position of the believer, while contrasting the experiences of Moses

---

[119] Strong, J. 1996. The exhaustive concordance of the Bible : Showing every word of the test of the common English version of the canonical books, and every occurrence of each word in regular order. (electronic ed.) (G4151). Woodside Bible Fellowship.: Ontario
[120] Luke 1.47 (NRSV) compared with (NCV)

and Israel with the New and Heavenly, or spiritual Jerusalem. It refers to Old Testament saints, whose salvation had now been made complete, because Christ had died as the Lamb of God, and had taken away the sin of the world.[121]

While it does declare that the spirits of these just men have been made perfect, it does not necessarily mean that these men are 'immortal beings', who have survived death. It only says that they have been made perfect. They have been made perfect, because they retrospectively share in the salvation that Christ brought through his death.

It is also possible that this use of the word *spirit* refers to the indivisible part of man, which was closely linked with the idea of the soul or *nephesh*, which was sometimes used in synonymous fashion with spirit. In this passage, *spirit* was possibly used to describe that part of the inner man or *nephesh* that is more closely concerned with God consciousness. These ideas can be suggested because of the way in which the interchangeable, and synonymous use of metaphorical language, helps to express certain ideas.

This was apparent in Paul's use of the word *pneuma*, as noted by Ladd. "The central term for humanity in the Old Testament, in the intertestamental literature, and in the rabbis was *nephesh* or *psuche*. In

---

[121] McGee, J. V. 1997, c1981. *Thru the Bible commentary*. Based on the Thru the Bible radio program. (electronic ed.) (5:608). Thomas Nelson: Nashville

Paul, it was *pneuma*. 'Spirit' has made a dramatic advance, *psuche* a dramatic retreat."[122] Ladd goes on to quote Stacey, who did not see this as the result of Hellenistic influences. Paul's experience with the Holy Spirit had influenced his anthropology, and *Pneuma* was now taking the lead role.[123]

While Paul used *pneuma* about 150 times, only a small number of these referred to man, and there was no suggestion of natural immortality. He did not seem "to coin his terms with reference to any anthropological ideas, but for a different purpose. He seems not to care about the question of a dipartite or tripartite anthropology, and his use of terms might not even implicitly entail or presuppose any anthropological ideas of that kind."[124]

This is exemplified in Romans 1:9, where Paul states that he served God with his *pneuma*. The word suggests a spirit of service in the sense that, "it was not that of a religious drudge, going through endless rituals and reciting prayers and liturgies by rote."[125] This use of *pneuma* was also apparent in 1 Corinthians 5:3, where Paul says, "Though absent in body, I am present in spirit; and as if present I have already pronounced

---

[122] George Eldon Ladd, A Theology of the New Testament. (Em. B. Eerdmans Publishing Co, Michigan, 1993), 503
[123] Ladd, 503
[124] Troels Engberg-Pedersen, Paul beyond the Judaism/Hellenism divide, (Westminster John Knox Press, 2001), 191
[125] MacDonald, W., & Farstad, A.,Believer's Bible Commentary (Ro 1:9)

judgment."[126] Obviously, Paul did not visit in an out of body experience, but the spiritual authority of Paul to command church discipline was there. He reinforced this in the following verse when he said, "My spirit is present with the power of our Lord Jesus."[127]

In the next verse after that, Paul's use of *pneuma* could suggest an immaterial part of man, when he says that the Church should hand over a man "to Satan for the destruction of the flesh, so that his spirit may be saved in the day of the Lord."[128] However, that the spirit may be saved in the day of the Lord, also suggests that it may not be saved. If it is not to be saved, then what happens to it? Therefore, Paul is not necessarily suggesting any type of post-mortem existence. This is because there is no evidence that the spirit that is not saved will continue to exist in an afterlife state. In fact, Paul never seems to suggest that man survives death apart from a body. This is an important idea that will be explored in a later chapter.

The phrase, *destruction of the flesh,* might mean that the act of excommunication was a form of punishment, sufficient to destroy whatever power of influence the flesh had over behaviour. In other words, this man was judged in the flesh that he might live. This use of *pneuma* may also be Paul's attempt to contrast the natural man against the importance of the spiritual

---

[126] 1 Corinthians 5:3 (NRSV)
[127] 1 Corinthians 5:4 (NRSV)
[128] 1 Corinthians 5:5 (NRSV)

man. Therefore, he could say, "Walk by the Spirit, and you will not gratify the desires of the flesh."[129]

In 1 Corinthians 2:11 Paul says, "What human being knows what is truly human except the human spirit that is within?"[130] This verse indicates that the human spirit is closely linked with being human, and therefore Paul could also say, "Be renewed in the spirit of your mind."[131] These verses suggest that *pneuma* expresses or describes an element of the mind or *psuche*.

In 1 Corinthians 14, Paul taught about praying in the spirit. He complained that if he prayed in a tongue, his mind was unproductive, and his solution was to suggest that the one praying interprets.[132] If the spirit could pray and the mind be left uninformed, this might suggest that the spirit is significantly differentiated from the self. However, in this case the only reason the mind is left uninformed, is that speaking in a tongue or another language would not be understood. Therefore, while one might speak in another tongue, the interpretation from the Holy Spirit would provide the understanding, by operating through the mind of the interpreter. These passages suggest that man's *pneuma* operates in close association with the natural capacities of man.

Considering these examples of Paul's use of

---

129 Galatians 5:16 (ESV)
130 1 Corinthians 2:11 (NRSV)
131 Ephesians 4:23 (NASB)
132 1 Corinthians 14:14

*pneuma*, it remains difficult to differentiate the *pneuma* from the man himself. The use of *pneuma* to describe intangible elements, or aspects of human nature, suggests that the human spirit that Paul talks about is the God conscious part of the physiological self. If Scripture were expected to define the spirit of man as a distinct and immortal part of man, then Paul's use of the word creates problems.

Whatever our understanding of the metaphysical makeup of man, it is the Holy Spirit that transforms his nature. In John 3:8, Jesus says that the wind (*pneuma*) blows where it wishes, and so is everyone who is born of the Spirit (*pneuma*). *Pneuma* could be translated as spirit in the first part of this verse, but context and the use of synonymous parallelism suggests the use of wind. The idea is that the Spirit operates on man in a way that is synonymous with the nature of wind. It suggests a change in man's condition that is a direct outcome of the activity of the Spirit within the believer.

For Nicodemus, Pharisee and leader of the Jews, the surprising news from Jesus was that the Kingdom of God involved "forces and transformations far beyond human capacities or human understanding alone."[133] We are born by the *pneuma* of God,[134] which

---

[133] Leland Ryken, et al, Dictionary of biblical imagery, (InterVarsity Press, 1998) 391
[134] John 3:6

dwells in us,[135] joining us with the Lord as one *pneuma*,[136] making us sons of God,[137] and members of the body of Christ.[138] The activity of God's *pneuma* on man suggests that a change in the nature of man is necessary, to enable him to operate as one *pneuma* with the Lord.

It is important to note that Paul described the church joined to the Lord as one spirit. The emphasis here is a unique relationship, created by the working of the Spirit of God. Being born again means that man's fundamental nature is changed, enabling him to become spiritually connected. It is an act of renewed spirituality, which manifests itself in new levels of God cognizance.

Therefore, Paul could say, "The Spirit Himself bears witness with our spirit that we are children of God."[139] In 1 Corinthians 2:12, Paul says, "We have received not the spirit of the world, but the Spirit that is from God, so that we may understand the gifts bestowed on us by God."[140] A few verses later, he says, "Those who are unspiritual do not receive the gifts of God's Spirit."[141] The gifts are spiritually discerned and understood by those with the *pneuma* of God.

---

[135] Romans 8:9
[136] 1 Corinthians 6:17
[137] Romans 8:14
[138] 1 Corinthians 12:13
[139] Romans 8:16 (NKJV)
[140] 1 Corinthians 2:12 (NRSV)
[141] 1 Corinthians 2:14 (NRSV)

Therefore, it is the Spirit of God that enables the *pneuma* of man to be spiritual, and although 1 Corinthians 2:11 states that man has *pneuma* within, there is no indication that the *pneuma* is separable from the man himself.

Ladd agrees with Bultmann's view that the *pneuma* is the person's true inner self, used to represent the self-consciousness as a willing and knowing self. He goes on to state that "The reception of the divine *pneuma* means the renewal of the human *pneuma*, so that it acquires new dimensions."[142]

Scripture suggests a modified anthropological state for the believer, but it is the presence and activity of God's Spirit in union and relationship with man that determines new birth and life. Conversely, Scripture seems to suggest that without the Holy Spirit there is no life. For example, Paul says, "The first man Adam became a living being; the last Adam became a life-giving spirit."[143] A paraphrased translation of Romans 8.10 says, "The Spirit gives you life because you have been made right with God."[144]

Because the Spirit of God is active in creating life, Paul could also say, "If the Spirit of Him who raised Jesus from the dead dwells in you, He who raised Christ Jesus from the dead *will also give life to your mortal*

---

[142] Ladd, 504-505
[143] 1 Corinthians 15:45 (ESV)
[144] Romans 8.10 (NLT)

*bodies* through his Spirit who dwells in you."[145] While this body is death,[146] the promise was the redemption of our bodies.[147] For example, Paul writes, "He will transform the body of our humiliation, that it may be conformed to the body of his glory, by the power that also enables him to make all things subject to himself."[148]

We only have life because the Spirit of God dwells in us, and importantly, our mortal selves are the recipients of this life. Man must be mortal, because any future existence is conditional on the life that God gives through his Holy Spirit. These ideas are also supported by Paul's teaching that only God has immortality.[149]

When Jesus appeared to his disciples after his resurrection, they were terrified because they believed they had seen a spirit.[150] To prove that he was not a spirit, he invited them to examine physical evidence of his death and asked for food. The reason for their immediate response was the assumption that they had seen a ghost.

The word used here was *pneuma*,[151] which is unusual because the general use of this word in the New Testament does not suggest the idea of a spectre.

---

[145] Romans 8:11 (NASB)
[146] Romans 7:24
[147] Romans 8:23
[148] Philippians 3:21 (NRSV)
[149] 1 Tim 6:16
[150] Luke 24:37
[151] Some translations use the word *Ghost*

The writer could have used *phantasma*,[152] which would have been more useful in describing a ghostly apparition.

While the use of *pneuma* does suggest something more ethereal, Jesus' response was important, because he did not focus on the supernatural. His interest lay in the physical. He was insistent that a ghost does not have a body, a statement that could not support the idea of an immortal soul existing after death, because the proof of life was dependent on a body.

Jesus had died, had been raised back to life in a solid body, and there was no evidence that he had existed or survived in a more ethereal state. Jesus only came back to life when his body was resurrected, and this makes him the firstborn[153] (*prototokos*) from the dead. Because he is the prototype for all that follow, our existence is intrinsically linked to the pattern that has been set, and it is the *Pneuma* of the Lord that guarantees the fulfilment of this pattern.

These ideas are evident in Paul's hope that he would not be found naked when his earthly tent was destroyed.[154] His understanding that any existence required a bodily form, explains why he earnestly desired to be clothed with the habitation, which is from heaven.[155] This emphasis on the restoration of the body

---

[152] In Matthew 14:26 the disciples call Jesus a *phantasma* as he walks across the water.
[153] Colossians 1:18
[154] 2 Corinthians 5:1-4
[155] 2 Corinthians 5:2 (NKJV)

after death, as the eschatological fulfilment of the life that God promises to those that believe, requires the careful consideration of the use of spirit and soul.

The interplay on the use of the words Spirit, wind, breath and life, and the similarity with the essential attributes of the soul, combined with the diffuse and varied teaching on the nature of both, makes it difficult to be dogmatic about the nature of man. The imagery cannot be missed. In Genesis, God created man and breathed the breath of life into him. In the same way, the believer received the *Pneuma* of God and was made alive. The opposite of this life was always death.

# Death and Life!

In the Old Testament, the death of man was generally seen as the complete end of his existence. However, while both good and bad went to the grave, the possibility of a rescue from death was hinted at in various places. For example, "The Lord kills and makes alive; He brings down to the grave and brings up."[156]

This rescue seemed to involve a bodily return to life, as suggested by Job, who believed that after his skin was destroyed, he would see God in his flesh.[157] Because his hope was in a physical restoration of his complete self, it would be illogical to believe that Job hoped in immediate life after death as an immortal being, because that would have been contradictory to his expressed hope. Likewise, the Psalmist expected that God would not allow his body to become corrupted in the grave; a statement that would double as a messianic reference of the future resurrection of Christ.[158]

The hope of avoiding the corruption of the body in the grave, explains why there was no clear or explicit expectation of some immediate post mortem existence. Life was something that was experienced in bodily

---

[156] 1 Samuel 2:6 (NKJV)
[157] Job 19:25-27
[158] Psalm 16:9-11

form. The loss of the body was man's fear, and the restoration of the body was the hope.

This link between the corruption of the body and the life of the person, is an essential element in understanding the Hebrew hope of rescue from the grave. Death as defined in Genesis remained man's ultimate enemy, and the undoing of death required a restoration of the physical self. While the hope was to avoid this corruption and to return to life, it was understood that the body would 'sleep in the dust' until 'woken up'.[159] This was a nice way of affirming the dissolution of man's body back to its essential elements, while expressing the hope of its restoration in the resurrection.

In the New Testament, the possibility of life after death was a significant issue. However, there was no explicit teaching that the soul or spirit survived the body at death, or that man was in some way naturally immortal. This is because the nature of death as an outcome of sin, is contradicted by the view that an immortal component of man lives on unaffected by death.

In addition, the emphasis of Scripture was on explaining the benefits of the believer's relationship with God. The believer was always dependent on God if he was to avoid death, an idea often brought out in Jesus' teaching. For example, "God so loved the world

---

[159] Daniel 12.2

that He gave His only begotten Son, that whoever believes in Him shall not perish (or die[160]), but have eternal life."[161]

Why use the word perish when die could be used? In some ways perish is actually a better translation, although die is equally useful. The problem of course with perish is that it has a number of different meanings. We could say all perished when the plane crashed, or we could say that the tyre perished under the hot sun. Either way, the idea is the demise of the subject. Other ways in which the word could be translated include – be put out of the way entirely, be abolished, be rendered useless, be killed, be put to death, be lost, be ruined and be destroyed.[162]

The emphasis was on the complete and total loss of the individual through being destroyed. This word was used by John, who quotes Caiaphas, who was the "one who had advised the Jews that it was better to have one person *die* for the people."[163]

The reason for the use of the word perish stems back to Greek grammar. Perish (*apoletai*) comes from *apollumi* meaning *to destroy*, and has been modified from its original verbal form. In this verse, it is in the middle voice, which makes the subject the recipient of the action described by the verb. In this case, we could

---

[160] The Good News Bible
[161] John 3:16 (NASB)
[162] Strong, J. (1996).
[163] John 18:14 (NRSV)

say he *was destroyed*. However, to complicate matters, this verb is also in the subjunctive form, which further modifies the use of the original word. In the following chart, we can see the evolution of the word from its root to its final modified form.

| Aorist | Normally, an undefined event occurring in the past. | ...he destroyed |
| Middle voice | Subject is the recipient of the action described by the verb. | ... he was destroyed |
| Subjunctive | Expresses an action that has not yet occurred. | ...he should not be destroyed.[164] |

This verse is also divided by *hina* (a conjunction translated by the word *that*), which in the subjunctive can indicate purpose and conditional possibilities.

| Purpose: | Salvation | For God so loved the world that he gave his only Begotten Son... |
| Condition: | Believing | Whoever believes... |
| Possibilities: | Death or life. | He Shall not die (be destroyed) but have everlasting life. |

---

[164] "The use of "should" confuses some English readers here because the English word "should" connotes a degree of doubtfulness, as if the text said "should not perish, but maybe he will." The Greek text contains no such connotation here; "should" has no directly corresponding equivalent word in the underlying Greek text, but is used in rendering the verb "perish," to represent the subjunctive mood (aorist tense, middle voice, third person singular) of the original. The subjunctive mood in Greek does not express, as in English, doubtfulness or "conditions contrary to fact," and can be used, in fact, in the strongest possible antithesis to doubtfulness in strong denial" Smith, J. H. 1992;

The use of destruction to describe the end of man, is synonymous with the Old Testament view of sin leading to death through the decomposition of the body. This verse shows that life is conditional on the life that God gives, and the contrasting possibilities are death or life. This idea is reinforced by Jesus' teaching on life and death in a number of verses, where he says that whoever believes in him will live even if they die.

*Truly, truly, I say to you, whoever hears my word and believes him who sent me has eternal life. He does not come into judgment, but has passed from death to life.*[165]

The last phrase of the verse shows us that the judgment that the believer avoids is death. It could be argued that Jesus was talking about a change from spiritual death to spiritual life, and that he was not talking about a physical death. The problem with this is that Jesus was very clear about the nature of death.

*Your fathers ate the manna in the wilderness, and they died. This is the bread that comes down from heaven, so that one may eat of it and not die.*[166]

Israel had been fed with manna, which sustained them for 40 years in the wilderness, and this bread had kept them alive, but it did not prevent them from

---

[165] John 5:24 (ESV)
[166] John 6:49-50 (ESV)

eventually dying in the desert. The problem of course is that believers still die a physical death. However, the promise that Jesus makes, is that *even* though we die we shall live, but only through the resurrection as explained in John 11:25-26.

> *Jesus said to her, "I am the resurrection and the life. Whoever believes in me, though he die, yet shall he live, and everyone who lives and believes in me shall never die. Do you believe this?"*[167]

Jesus is the resurrection and the life. Jesus does not come to offer the hope that even though we die we will continue to exist *beyond* the grave. His promise is that we will return *from* the grave, a place where the dead are dead. This point is made clear to Martha on the death of her brother Lazarus, whom Jesus raised from the dead. The return of the dead to life is a physical demonstration of the meaning of the message that Jesus proclaimed. Even though Lazarus died, he lives and the death that Lazarus returned from was not spiritual, but physical because he returned from the grave still wrapped in his burial clothes.

The contrasting possibilities and outcomes are framed by the condition of believing. If you believe, then even if you die you will live. If you do not believe then you will die and you will not live. The

---

[167] John 11:25-26 (ESV)

understanding here is synonymous with the creation story and the condition of obedience that would lead to life, and disobedience that would lead to death. In both the Old and New Testaments there is a clear picture of the conditional possibilities presented by contrasting choices, and in both cases, the consequence of not believing was death.

If man is subject to a judgment that was described by Jesus as death, then that makes him mortal. If man is mortal, then he must receive immortality if he is to avoid death, an idea reinforced by other passages of Scripture. For example, Paul stated that Jesus Christ had "abolished death and brought life and immortality to light through the gospel."[168]

A comparison of Paul's teaching[169] also shows that eternal life was equivalent to immortality and conversely, death was equivalent to mortality. These ideas reinforce the emphasis of the creation story, where disobedience led to the physical death of man.

However, the second Adam (Christ) gave up his life, abolished death, and gave man the opportunity to become immortal. If Jesus brought immortality through the gospel, then logic dictates that prior to the gospel, there was no immortality. The glimmer of hope that was expressed in the Old Testament, is finally and fully realised in Jesus. "For just as the Father raises the dead

---

[168] 2 Timothy 1:10 (NASB)
[169] 2 Corinthians 5:4, 1 Corinthians 15:53-54

and gives them life, even so the Son also gives life to whom He wishes."[170]

This verse is important, because it explains that being given life and being raised from the dead are synonymous terms. The dead are only given life when they are raised from the dead by the Father, which contradicts the idea that man naturally continues to exist beyond the grave. In other words, for man to receive life by being raised from the dead, he must actually be dead.

Although Scripture tends to emphasise the fact that only those raised from the dead are given life, there is also a resurrection that does not lead to life. This resurrection is the subject of another chapter. While Jesus explained the conditions by which eternal life might be gained, Paul provided a very detailed explanation of the metaphysical process.

Paul wrote that we do not want to be unclothed, but further clothed that mortality may be swallowed up by life (*zoe*).[171] The metaphor of being clothed was used by Paul to make the connection between eternal life and the provision of a body. For example, in verse 1-3 of the same chapter he stated that if "the earthly tent we live in is destroyed, we have a building from God, a house not made with hands, eternal in the heavens. For in this tent we groan, longing to be clothed with our heavenly

---

[170] John 5:21 (NASB).
[171] 2 Corinthians 5:4

dwelling, if indeed, when we have taken it off, we will not be found naked."[172]

These ideas were contrary to the Greek belief in the immortality of the soul, and they suggest that Paul believed that we would not be disembodied entities. Logic dictates that Paul understood that man is a mortal being, who needs to be re-clothed in a way that he is able to receive the *zoe* life that God promises. In other words, we only receive immortality when we are re-clothed and to be re-clothed we must receive new bodies and to receive new bodies there must be a resurrection.

In 1 Corinthians 15:53, Paul says that this corruptible must put on incorruption, and this mortal must put on immortality. Again, it is very clear that Paul understands the nature of man to be mortal. He is mortal because he is corruptible and that his only chance is to put on immortality, which requires supernatural intervention.

In verse 54 of 1 Corinthians 15, Paul goes on to say that when this mortal has put on immortality, then death is swallowed up in victory. Therefore, immortality is something that the believer receives in substitution for his mortality, and once this happens death no longer has any power. Death no longer has any power because immortality has been granted.

The use of parallelism between immortality,

---

[172] 2 Corinthians 5:1-3 (NRSV)

death, corruption and incorruption, helps to explain that immortality means to be free from the possibility of corruption.[173] The emphasis on being free from corruption only makes sense if death is the end of man, and the resurrection to a state of immortality in a new incorruptible body is the hope. If man only becomes immortal because God's plan is to transform him by raising him from the dead, then for this to happen he must actually be dead. It is from this state of death that we will receive a resurrection body.

In addition, it is unlikely that the body that we are re-clothed in will be an exact reconstitution of our bodies from the original molecules. Paul said that we would not be unclothed, but further clothed,[174] and that flesh and blood could not inherit incorruption.[175] It is logically apparent that our bodies are constantly replacing and repairing cells from what we eat and drink. Most of the human body is water, which is replaced many times over in a lifetime. Cells die and are past out and replaced. The steak that I eat becomes part of my body for a while, but not a permanent part of me.

Therefore, if death is the dissolution of man back to dust because he is a mortal being who cannot inherit incorruption, then it cannot be the dust that is brought back to reconstitute the individual. It has no part in the

---

[173] 1 Corinthians 15:50-54
[174] 2 Corinthians 5:4
[175] 1 Corinthians 15:50

incorruptible state of existence that is promised in the resurrection to eternal life, where we will be clothed in a new and incorruptible body.

It is also unlikely that my soul is waiting in heaven to be reunited with my new body, because the body was the vehicle to immortality. Paul's teaching on the importance of a new body in the resurrection supports these ideas. For example, in 1 Corinthians 15:35-41, he taught that the physical body is sown in death, but is raised a spiritual body.[176] We will be changed in the resurrection from death to life in a new body. There will be a connection with our past life and yet we will be different.

To explain this idea, Paul used the imagery of a seed to make the before and after connection. The seed that is planted dies, but what sprouts forth is different and yet inherently connected to the seed it came from. This could be comparable to the way in which the DNA in the seed is the pattern for the form of the plant that grows.

He then built on this idea by explaining that there are different types of celestial and terrestrial bodies. In a similar way, our resurrection bodies will somehow differ from our earthly bodies. In verses 42-43, he reverted again to the concept of a seed. The body is sown in corruption, raised in incorruption. The body is sown in dishonour, raised in glory. The body is sown

---

[176] 1 Corinthians 15:44

in weakness, it is raised in power. The body is sown a natural body, it is raised a spiritual body.

Then Paul goes on to make the connection between the first Adam and the Last Adam (Christ). The first Adam was made of dust. However, the second Adam, the spiritual Man is from heaven. We inherited our nature from the First Adam and being made of dust, so we too are like him - also being made of dust. In the resurrection, we will be made in the form of the Heavenly Man.

The resurrection therefore transforms the Christian body into the body bearing the image of the man from heaven, who is Christ. It is important to note that the mechanism for immortality that Paul describes is the physical resurrection of the dead. The resurrection not only brings a transformation or further clothing, it also brings us back from a place of being dead.

Of course, all this requires the supernatural intervention of God's power to change and transform us, to which Paul refers to as a mystery.[177] Paul makes the important conclusion that we will all be changed, and death will be swallowed up in victory.[178] In other words, Death will only be defeated when we are raised to life in new bodies.

Paul also extends the mystery to the possibility

---

[177] 1 Corinthians 15:51
[178] 1 Corinthians 15:54

that not everyone will die, and that some will be alive at the return of Christ. This is because Paul teaches that the resurrection event is the climax of God's redemptive purposes for the Church at the end of the age. In both 1 Thessalonians 4 and 1 Corinthians 15, Paul described how those who remained until the coming of the Lord[179] would be transformed,[180] and would not experience death or resurrection. However, those who had previously died, the dead in Christ would be both raised from the dead and be transformed.[181]

It is important to note that Paul points out that those who are alive at the return of Christ, will in no way precede those who had previously died.[182] After the resurrection, those who are still alive at the Lord's return will be caught up in the air with them.

If the dead are resurrected to join those alive at the return of Christ, then they must have remained dead until that event. If they remained dead until that point, it is also unlikely that they existed as immortal souls awaiting new bodies. This is because such an idea was contrary to the emphasis placed on a new body in the resurrection, which would enable man to become immortal. While those who were still alive at the return of Christ are not resurrected, Paul states that they will

---

[179] 1 Thessalonians. 4:15
[180] 1 Corinthians 15:51
[181] 1 Corinthians 15:52
[182] 1 Thessalonians 4:15

be transformed.[183] The word 'transformed' (*allasso*) can mean to exchange one thing for another. The idea here is that those alive at the return of Christ still need new bodies to obtain immortality.

The passages in Thessalonians and Corinthians clearly suggest that the believer does not depart for heaven at death. While Paul does talk about departing this life to be with the Lord as a more attractive alternative,[184] this only serves to reinforce Paul's hope in the resurrection. Therefore, Paul used the word sleep as a metaphor for death. It presents the view that death is for the believer an event from which they will awaken. This is not the sleep as we know it in the sense of an individual's unconscious passage of time. Any form of conscious or unconscious existence cannot be death. In this case, death does not represent something to be feared, because for the believer it is like a sleep.[185]

Although the Physical death for the believer is still a reality, it is through the resurrection from the dead that he receives immunity from eternal death, when he is raised as an incorruptible being, transformed and re-clothed in a new body.

In addition, if man does not survive death apart from a body, then what comes back from death must be the individual whom God remembers. This was the expectation of Job who observed that like the river that

---

[183] 1 Corinthians 15:52
[184] Philippians 1:23
[185] 1 Thessalonians 4:14 (NKJV)

has dried up, man lies down and does not rise again;[186] but then goes on to express the hope that somehow God would remember him in his death. "Oh that you would hide me in Sheol, that you would conceal me until your wrath be past, that you would appoint me a set time, and remember me!"[187]

Therefore, it seems likely that between death and the resurrection, I actually do not exist, and yet I am somehow kept safe by the knowledge and power of God. It is only after this supernatural intervention that we are made truly immortal, and the pattern for this resurrection is Christ, who is the first fruits of those who have fallen asleep.

---

[186] Job 14:12 (ESV)
[187] Job 14:13 (ESV)

# An Intermediate State?

One of our initial questions concerning the nature of man was whether he naturally survived death as an immortal being. In the Genesis creation narrative, man died through disobedience and that death was carefully defined as the dissolution of the body. There was no mention of what happened to man after death. By contrast, the idea of the natural immortality of man raises the possibility of an intermediate state, which might exist between death and the resurrection. From Paul's teaching, this seems very unlikely, but it is still important to examine all the issues. What does the rest of Scripture say about the period between death and any possible future existence?

In Psalm 6:5 it says, "In death there is no remembrance of you; in *Sheol* who can give you praise?"[188] Throughout the Old Testament, the word *sheol* is sometimes left un-translated and sometimes the word grave is used. Sometimes it is translated by the English word hell. However, the concept of hell, influenced by extra-biblical mythology, does not correspond to a scriptural definition of *sheol*. From its use in various contexts, it would appear that *sheol* is the grave.

---

[188] Psalm 6:5 (NRSV)

The Psalmist says that in death, no one will remember God, and he rhetorically asks who can give God praise. The rhetorical nature of the question suggests that the writer is making the point that there is no one in *sheol* to give praise. To suggest otherwise would contradict the purpose of rhetorical questions; which are used without expectation of a reply, because the answer should be obvious. In this case, the answer is made even more obvious by the previous statement that the dead would not remember God. It is not likely that those in *sheol* are incapable of remembering God. Rather, the rhetorical nature of the Psalmist's comment simply suggests that praise and cognisance are elements of the living and not the dead.

The idea that death leads to a loss of existence was a familiar theme in the Old Testament. Job compared those going down to the grave as a cloud that fades and vanishes. Those who went down to *sheol* did not come back up because they ceased to exist.[189] In Psalm 88:11, these ideas are supported in rhetorical fashion. "Shall your loving kindness be declared in the grave? Or Your faithfulness in the place of destruction?"[190] In this verse, the grave is synonymous with destruction. If the grave is a place of destruction, then it is unlikely that anyone actually has any form of existence, and therefore they are not in a position to

---

[189] Job 7:9
[190] Psalm 88:11 (NKJV)

remember God.

In Isaiah 14:11, it says that those brought down to *sheol* have the maggots as a bed beneath them, and worms as their covering. This suggests that the grave is the end of man, because he is destroyed through the process of decomposition, confirming the Genesis story that the consequence of sin was the dissolution of the body back to dust.

While David described the sorrows of *sheol* surrounding him,[191] the full context explains that this passage was about David's deliverance from the hand of Saul. David was not saying that he was in *sheol* suffering, but rather that he was close to death, and yet God had rescued him. This is supported by David's acknowledgement that in his distress, he cried out to God, and the Lord had heard him.

Context is always important in our understanding of the use of the word *sheol*. For example, in the rebellion and judgment of Korah,[192] it says that they went down alive into *sheol*, and yet afterwards it says that they perished when the earth closed down over them. In this case, the idea of going into *sheol* was the equivalent of being buried alive.

The emphasis of Scripture is that *sheol* is a gloomy non-descriptive end to the life of man. Job melancholically states, "Shall we have rest together in

---

[191] 2 Samuel 22:6
[192] Numbers 16:30 (NRSV)

the dust?"[193] The rhetorical nature of the question expects no answer, because it is obvious that it is not possible to rest if you are dust. Many passages reflect on *sheol* in the context of the fear or danger of death that surrounds oneself, and the sorrow and trouble that it presents. The hope was always deliverance from *sheol* or the grave, and to live again in the land of the living. In Psalm 116:3-9, the Psalmist says that the pains of death and the pangs of Sheol are laying hold of him and bringing him trouble and sorrow. His response was to call on the Name of the Lord for help, which enabled him to joyfully declare the expectation that his soul would be delivered from death. His hope was that he would eventually walk before the Lord in the land of the living.

There was no sense that man expected to exist in any shape or form in *sheol*. It was a place of 'nothingness' and something from which to be rescued. "For the living know that they will die, but the dead know nothing, and they have no more reward, for the memory of them is forgotten."[194]

However, the hope was that God would be able to defeat the power of the grave and rescue man from its clutches. As the Psalmist says, "God will redeem my soul from the power of *sheol*."[195] The Teaching of the Old Testament is that man understands his final

---

[193] Job 17:16 (NKJV)
[194] Ecclesiastes 9:5 (ESV)
[195] Psalm 49:15 (NASB)

destination is the grave and a state of existence, which is the antithesis of a life to which he hopes to return.

There are no scriptures in the Old Testament that clearly and consistently detail conscious existence after death in an intermediate state. While there are a small number of New Testament passages that might seem to support the idea of an intermediate state of existence, there are a number of issues to consider. Sound theology is built on a consistent framework of scriptures that confirm ideas in a way that are understandable and useful. In particular, some passages are used to promote certain interpretations, even though they are not consistent with Scripture.

When other scriptures contradict or contrast these more consistent ideas, then there are likely to be interpretive issues that require special consideration. The most obvious example is the story of the Rich Man and Lazarus.[196] In this story, the fortunes of a rich man and a poor man are reversed in death; the rich man is suffering in *hades* and the poor man is enjoying life in 'Abraham's bosom'.

There are a number of problems with this story if it is a valid description of an intermediate stage. The first problem is that the story takes place in *hades,*[197] which is emptied of its dead and thrown into the lake

---

[196] Luke 16

[197] *Sheol* (the grave in the Old Testament) and *hades* were seen to be equivalent because Peter quotes the Old Testament using hades in place of *sheol*. Acts 2:27 and Psalm 16:10

of fire after the final judgment.[198] This means that it cannot be a place of conscious existence. The other problem with this story is also the very thing that ironically seems to give it credibility – a description of the afterlife. The argument might be that this detailed story must describe after death circumstances. It must have been told to reinforce a reality for which all will experience.

However, whereas this circular reasoning might seem to give credibility to this interpretation, this descriptive view of the afterlife actually contradicts Scripture. Besides the fact that Scripture tells us that *hades* is only full of dead people, there are no other supporting passages. The vivid nature of the story would almost certainly have required some form of commentary or response from other writers. However, there were no comments from any of the New Testament writers on this passage. There was no teaching anywhere that supported the idea that the grave was divided into pleasant and unpleasant compartments, where the righteous and unrighteous could chat to one another.

Because the grave always had vague descriptive statements, the details of a story that has no other supporting commentary should be given careful consideration. If it was not consistent with Scripture, then it cannot be used to reinforce the viewpoint that

---

[198] Revelations 20:13,14

this was an accurate explanation of the afterlife.

It could be suggested then, that Jesus' use of this material in his story telling might be potentially misleading. However, there seems to have been no confusion to those who were listening because there was no response to the details. In response to this, an argument could be made that Jesus was reinforcing commonly held beliefs about the afterlife. The problem with this is that there was no uniform Jewish view on the nature of the afterlife.[199] Therefore, there would have been further teaching here and elsewhere in Scripture that supports the ideas in this story.

Jesus' teaching always focussed on life from death. It was never about being dead yet alive, which is what an intermediate state suggests. Genesis tells us that death was the dissolution of self, which by inference is the end of existence. If Jesus taught that we rise from the dead to receive life, then it is illogical to accept that the dead are still alive awaiting this event. It is very clear from New Testament teaching that the resurrection was foundational to Christian belief. Paul was adamant that the dead rose from the dead in new bodies to receive eternal life.

Therefore, this passage was contradictory to teaching on the resurrection. It generated no theological discussion and did not appear to have been used to support a particular view of the afterlife. Then why

---

[199] Fudge, The Fire That Consumes, 154

would Jesus tell this story if it was not a vivid depiction of the afterlife, and a reality that all would get to experience?

The answer is that there was nothing surprising about what Jesus was saying, because they had heard this sort of story before. Jesus often spoke in parables, which always had a key point that often summarised a previous debate or issue with either his disciples, the crowds of people that came to hear him speak or the religious leaders of the day. When Jesus spoke in parables, he used common everyday familiar objects and concepts. It should be no surprise then to learn that the plot of this story was familiar in popular Palestinian stories of Jesus' time.

Hugo Gressman says that there were at least seven versions of this story in Jewish literature. "The plot of the parables, the reversal of Earthly fortunes after death, was familiar in Palestinian popular stories of Jesus' time.....One of the most famous Involved a poor student of the Law and a rich publican named Bar Ma'jan."[200]

Its use was summed up by Froom, who cites the historian Josephus and concludes, "Jesus was clearly using a then common tradition of the Jews to press home a moral lesson in a related field."[201] It suggests that the story was a means to an end and the

---

[200] Fudge, The Fire That Consumes, 203-204
[201] Fudge, The Fire That Consumes, 204

background details are not as important as the point being made by the story. Jesus' use of this story would be recognized not in terms of its content, but in terms of its message. The Pharisees would have been expecting the punch line at the end of the story, which was the meaning of the parable.

The important details were that the favoured man was rich, the beggar was poor, and there was a reversal of circumstances in death. The context in which this story was told is also important. Jesus had been teaching about faithfulness and he used stewardship to reinforce the concept. The Pharisees who loved money, scoffed at Jesus' teaching, and therefore he told this story of the reversal of fortunes for one that was rich and one that was poor.

The reversal of circumstances in the light of Jesus' ministry becomes essential to understanding the story. Considering all of Jesus' numerable warnings to the Pharisees and the Nation of Israel,[202] it is possible that the reversal of circumstances in this story is also a portrayal of events that would soon befall them.

The rich man in the story could represent the Jewish nation who had enjoyed all of God's favour and goodness. The beggar would represent the gentiles who stood spiritually neglected at the gate of Israel. The rich man had failed to be a good steward of the riches at his disposal, and likewise, Israel had failed to be a

---

[202] See next Chapter on the Judgment of Israel

good steward of God's promises. In death, their circumstances are reversed, and now the beggar is the favoured one.

This story was a warning of the coming Judgment of Israel and the opportunity for the Gentiles to receive the Gospel. Death defined the finality of the events. The story also pointed out that even if someone were to come back from the dead the wicked would still not believe; therefore, the fortunes of Israel would be reversed, and even a resurrection from the dead would not be enough to prevent this reversal.

This is the punch line that Jesus made at the end of the story when he says, "If they do not hear Moses and the prophets, neither will they be persuaded though one rise from the dead."[203] Considering all these different ideas, means that it was very unlikely that Jesus had in mind a conscious state of existence in an intermediate state.

There are other scriptures such as 1 Peter 3:18-20, which described Christ preaching to the spirits in prison who were disobedient in the days of Noah, when eight were "saved through water."[204] This passage could be taken to mean that Jesus went into the realm of the dead to preach to Noah's contemporaries. He went there either to save them or to proclaim his own victory, but there are problems with these ideas.

---

[203] Luke 16:31 (NKJV)
[204] 1 Peter 3:18-20 (NKJV)

Firstly, there are no scriptures that suggest that one can be saved after death and secondly, why would Jesus need to proclaim his own victory? These two problems require us to carefully examine the interpretive issues.

If certain ideas are not confirmed in other scriptures, then we have to ask why? What was Peter trying to say? There are many different explanations and no clear interpretation for this passage. For example, one commentary notes, "The spirits in prison could refer to evil angels, to individuals who have died, or to the people who were alive at the time of Noah....the passage is difficult to interpret."[205]

If difficulties of interpretation exist, then the principles of interpretation suggest that this passage cannot be used to support theological views that might be considered normal. This is particularly relevant when those ideas are contradictory to other passages of Scripture.

There are clues as to what Peter might have been trying to say. Peter was keen to note that only eight people survived this flood, and then went on to make the connection between Noah's survival, baptism, and salvation. He wanted his readers to make the connection between the salvation of Noah and their own salvation in times of great wickedness. This makes

---

[205] Thomas Nelson, I. 1997, c1995. *Woman's Study Bible* . (1 Peter 3:18). Thomas Nelson: Nashville

sense because Peter had just been talking about suffering.

However, what was the wickedness that existed at the time of Noah? Seeking the answer to this question creates more problems. Genesis 6:1-5 says that people began to multiply and daughters were born, the sons of God took wives for themselves, the Nephilim were on the earth, the sons of God went in to the daughters of humans (who bore children to them) and the Lord saw that there was wickedness everywhere! Therefore, the flood was used to destroy everyone apart from Noah and his family.

These verses are equally difficult to explain. It is possible that Peter and his readers determined certain understandings from this passage that are not necessarily clear for us. Peter's allusion to the strange events in the antediluvian period may be his opportunity to demonstrate that God is able to destroy wickedness and keep evil in check.

But, this is not the only difficult passage from Peter. Consider 1 Peter 4:6, which says that the gospel was proclaimed even to the dead that they might live in the spirit as God does. This passage might seem to support the argument for the preaching of the gospel to the dead. However, sound Biblical interpretation looks for the overall scriptural emphasis. The consistent teaching of Scripture was that there was no second chance for the dead. It is more likely that Peter was simply saying that the gospel was proclaimed to those in the past. Before Christ, they had received the gospel through faith and had subsequently died. Even though they believed, they died because death remains a judgment in the flesh. The fact that they "might live in the spirit as God does," may mean that they will live again in their spiritually modified bodies, but this does not necessarily mean this has happened yet. Taking this sort of understanding into account, it is entirely possible that 1 Peter 3:18-20 refers to the preaching of the Gospel by Noah to his spiritually imprisoned contemporaries.

The idea of an intermediate state of existence is devoid of any consistent, clear, and specific teaching and we are limited to a few difficult passages. To build a theology of an intermediate state of existence relying on these passages also contradicts other scriptures.

The essential factor in these arguments is the nature of death. Genesis explained death as a consequence for sin without regard for any future existence, and therefore the possibility of life after death is only possible if the curse of death is overturned. This undoing of death is now fully realised and revealed in Christ, and death for the believer no longer holds any power. While we still die, God promises that those that have believed will rise from the grave to inherit eternal life.

There was no sense in this teaching that man continued to exist after death apart from the resurrection. This death was also often described as sleep, which was a nice way of talking about death. "We shall not all sleep, but we shall all be changed - in a moment, in the twinkling of an eye, at the last trumpet. For the trumpet will sound, and the dead will be raised incorruptible, and we shall be changed."[206] Comparing "we shall not all sleep" with "the dead will be raised," explains that this *sleep* is synonymous with *death.*[207]

The reason that some will not die or sleep is explained in 1 Thessalonians 4:15, where Paul tells us that those left alive at the return of Christ would have no advantage over those who had already died. The word *advantage* means that they would not *precede* or go before those who were already dead. In other words, the dead or those who had fallen asleep would be resurrected first before anything else. Then those who were still alive would be transformed. Therefore, those who had died must still be dead. The metaphor sleep describes how death for them will be an unconscious awareness of the period between their death and the resurrection.

The idea that man sleeps in the dust waiting for the resurrection as a fulfilment of promise, also seems to be confirmed by Daniel. "Many of those who sleep in the dust of the earth shall awake, some to everlasting

[206] 1 Corinthians 15:51 (NKJV)
[207] Besides the obvious parallelism in this verse, some versions also use die instead of sleep in the first part of the verse. "We shall not all die." (NRSV)

life, some to shame and everlasting contempt."[208] Further on it says, "Go your way till the end; for you shall rest, and will arise to your inheritance at the end of the days."[209] Therefore Man sleeps in the dust of the earth (which is death) to be awakened (at the resurrection) - some to receive an inheritance (to receive that which had been promised which is immortality) - the rest to everlasting contempt (which is a judgment of death). This 'sleep' of death is a very safe sleep for the believer is 'with Christ'[210] or 'asleep in Jesus'.[211] The use of the word sleep then provides a sense of security that God is in control. He will do what he has promised, and that we are not like those who have no hope.

These ideas are also supported by other passages. For example, Hebrews stated that the heroes of faith had died, and had not received the promises.[212] Later on, the writer notes, "Apart from us they should not be made perfect."[213] These passages suggest that they had not received what had been promised, because this would only happen when all were made perfect at the end of time. The only thing that would make them collectively perfect, would be the bodily resurrection of the dead, and an incorruptible body leading to immortality.

---

[208] Daniel 12:2
[209] Daniel 12:13 (NKJV)
[210] Philippians. 1:23
[211] 1 Corinthians 15:18
[212] Hebrews 11:13
[213] Hebrews 11:40 (NASB)

# The End of the Wicked

Scripture seems to emphasise the mortal nature of human beings, who totally depend on God to raise them from the dead if they are to live after dying. As previously stated, the resurrection from the dead is the mechanism by which this immortality is made available, when the perishable put on the imperishable.

While the lost or wicked will also be raised, what happens to them in this resurrection must differ greatly from the resurrection that leads to life. This is what Scripture suggests as in John 5:29, which described this as the resurrection of condemnation.[214] Romans 2:7-8 says that eternal life comes to those, who by patient continuance in doing good seek for glory, honour, and immortality; but those who are self-seeking, and do not obey the truth, they will receive indignation and wrath.[215]

The nature of this judgment or condemnation has caused considerable debate. Our understanding of immortality, whether it be conditional or natural, will influence our understanding on what happens to the wicked in this judgment. If man is naturally immortal and he is immune from death, then it follows that when

---

[214] John 5:28-29
[215] Romans 2:7-8 (NKJV)

he 'dies' he will continue to exist, albeit in another form. In these circumstances, the unjust or the wicked must also continue to exist forever. In this case, we should expect a judgment that reflects the status of their existence.

However, because immortality is immunity from death in new incorruptible bodies, Scripture suggests that the resurrection of the unjust is actually for the process of judgment leading to destruction (a second death). For example, Paul said that the wicked would be punished with everlasting destruction from the presence of the Lord.[216]

The idea of destruction for the unbeliever was also stated in John 3:16, where the word *perish* could be translated *die*. Therefore, death and destruction are equivalent terms used to describe the end of the wicked. This agrees with the judgment of man in Genesis, that his death would result in his destruction and that he would return to dust.

There are many other references in Scripture that described the end of the wicked in terms of destruction. In Psalm 9:5, it says that God had destroyed the wicked and blotted their name out forever. Psalm 21:9-10 says, "You shall make them as a fiery oven in the time of Your anger; The Lord shall swallow them up in His wrath, And the fire shall devour them. Their offspring You shall destroy from the earth, And their

---

[216] 2 Thessalonians 1:9 (NKJV)

descendants from among the sons of men."[217] "The messianic character of this Psalm is evident in that although the victory was completely David's, nevertheless ultimate victory comes only to the 'seed of David'."[218] Therefore, at least one commentary can note that this passage describes the doom of Christ's enemies at his return.[219]

David himself seemed to think of death as the end of man. In verse 1 of Psalm 28, he asked the Lord not to be silent lest he be like those who go down to the pit (*sheol/grave*), and then in verse 3, he asked the Lord not to take him away with the wicked, and then in verse 5 he says that the Lord will destroy the wicked. Therefore, David viewed the pit, the destination of the wicked, and their destruction in synonymous fashion. He did not want to become like those who go down to the pit, because David knew that the Lord would destroy them and not build them up.

In Psalm 59:13 it says, "Destroy them in your anger; destroy them completely!"[220] This Psalm of David under attack from his enemies might be understood as a temporal event. However, the nature of the language and the description of the fate of the wicked, without reference to any future existence, seems to support the idea that this destruction *is* the

---

[217] Psalm 21:9-10 (NKJV)
[218] *KJV Bible commentary*. 1997, c1994 (1006). Thomas Nelson: Nashville
[219] MacDonald, W., & Farstad, A., Believer's Bible Commentary (Ps 21:8)
[220] Psalm 59:13 (NCV)

end of their existence.

This theme of destruction for the wicked also finds its expression in various Hebrew words, which provide the nuance of meaning to the English word destroy. For example, the word *Shamad* always expressed complete 'destruction' or 'annihilation.'[221] Therefore, the Psalmist could say, "Wicked people grow like the grass. Evil people seem to do well, but they will be destroyed (*shamad*) forever."[222] This verse could also be translated *exterminated forever*, imagery which strongly suggests no possibility of any kind of future existence. This idea is reinforced by other passages such as Isaiah 26, which says, "They are dead, they will not live; They are deceased, they will not rise. Therefore You have punished and destroyed (*shamad*) them, And made all their memory to perish."[223]

Another word used to describe this destruction was *kalah*, which means that something ceases to be, perishes, or is completed. "Those who forsake the Lord shall be consumed (*kalah*)."[224] This word is translated die in the New Century Version, which in context described the outcome of that which is being consumed. When the word was used negatively, it could mean, "to make vanish" or "go away." *Kalah* was used in this sense in Deuteronomy 32:23, when God

---

[221] Vine, W. E., Unger, M. F., & White, W. 1996.
[222] Psalm 92:7 (NCV)
[223] Isaiah 26:14 (NKJV)
[224] Isaiah1:28 (NKJV).

says, "I will use (*Kalah*) my arrows on them."[225] In other words, all his arrows were gone - used up - vanished from his possession. Another example of this nuance is found in Job 7:9, which talks about the cloud that is consumed and vanishes away. Another negative nuance was to "destroy" something or someone as in "the famine shall consume the land."[226]

Therefore, the Bible expressed ideas that emphasized the end of the wicked in terms of non-existence. They will cease to be. They will be no more. "In a little while the wicked will be no more. You may look for them, but they will be gone."[227] This connection between destruction as a punishment and the loss of existence as an outcome of that punishment, strongly suggests that there could not have been any continuous form of existence in the afterlife for the wicked. For example, in Psalm 9:5 it says, "You spoke strongly against the foreign nations and destroyed (*abad*) the wicked; you wiped out their names forever and ever."[228] Because the word *abad* can mean perish, vanish, destroy, or exterminate,[229] the expectation of destruction for the wicked includes the idea that this destruction leads to a loss of existence. This idea is reinforced by the parallel statement in the final part of the verse. While the psalmist may have been troubled

---

[225] Deut. 32:23 (NASB)
[226] Gen. 41:30 (NKJV)
[227] Psalm 37:10 (NCV)
[228] Psalm 9:5 (NCV)
[229] Strong, J. (1996).

by his enemies, he was able to foresee that the very memory of them had perished, suggesting that they themselves are no more.[230]

This idea is further exemplified in Isaiah 1:28, which says that the transgressors would be consumed (*kalah*) - they would vanish, cease to exist, perish - and then a few verses later it tells us further about the outcome of the wicked. "The strong shall be as tinder, And the work of it as a spark; Both will burn together, And no one shall quench them."[231] The use of fire was often used to describe the destruction of the wicked or enemies who would be burnt up. In Psalm 97:3 it says, "A fire goes before him and burns up his enemies all around."[232] Commentaries on this verse suggest that the Psalmist uses poetic language in an attempt to describe the final judgment of God upon the earth before He establishes His kingdom;[233] and that the Lord will utterly destroy His enemies in the future Day of the Lord.[234] Malachi also described how God would arrive as a Judge and deal with the wicked who would be burnt up.[235] The imagery of this Great Day of the Lord carries on into the New Testament, where John the

---

[230] Psalm 9:6 (NCV)

[231] Isaiah 1:31 (NKJV)

[232] Psalm 97:3 (NCV)

[233] Radmacher, E. D., Allen, R. B., & House, H. W. 1997. *The Nelson study Bible : New King James Version*. Includes index. (Ps 97:3). T. Nelson Publishers: Nashville

[234] MacArthur, J. J. 1997, c1997. *The MacArthur Study Bible* (electronic ed.) (Ps 97:3). Word Pub.: Nashville

[235] Malachi 4:1

Baptist declared, "Every tree that does not produce good fruit will be cut down and thrown into the fire."[236]

The language of Scripture is constantly regular in its expectation of the fate for the wicked. "Through the wrath of the LORD of hosts the land is scorched, and the people are like fuel for the fire; no one spares another."[237] Fire is a vivid metaphor for destruction for it totally consumes. There was no mention of any expectation of some future existence for the wicked, because the judgments accentuate the loss of personal participation in life. Therefore, the judgments describe a punishment complete within itself. This idea is supported by Peter who made the connection between the destruction of all mankind in the flood, and a coming judgment by fire.[238] The comparison suggests that Peter imagined the complete end of the wicked, without thought of future existence.

These ideas are also reinforced by Isaiah, who says that not only will they die in a fire that will be unquenchable, but that their bodies will also be consumed by worms.[239] This verse was also quoted in the New Testament to support teaching on the judgment of *gehenna*, which is usually translated by the word *hell*.[240] While the worm does not die and the fires are not quenched, the bodies are dead. The wicked are

---

[236] Matthew 3:10 (NCV)
[237] Isaiah 9:19 (ESV)
[238] 2 Peter 3:5-7
[239] Isaiah 66:24
[240] Mark 9:48 quoted from Isaiah 66:24

corpses who are dead, and this fits the picture of a burning rubbish heap complete with maggots. It is a vivid description of judgment, but there was no suggestion at any stage that those in *gehenna* continued to exist.

Furthermore, the origins of *gehenna* supports the idea that it was a place of destruction. Gehenna actually referred to one of the principal valleys outside Jerusalem, named Valley of the Son of Hinnom. The 'fire of Gehenna' had developed from historical events, which in time meant that this valley came to be associated with the destiny of the wicked. For example, Jeremiah had described how the people had established a site for sacrificing children to the god Molech, which ironically would become a dump for their own corpses. The nature of this judgment as an act of destruction was made clear by Jeremiah, who stated that the dead bodies would be food for the birds of the air and the beasts of the earth.[241]

While the possibility that Gehenna described a place of punishment in the afterlife might be suggested by some intertestamental literature shortly before 100 BC, "the place is unnamed *and* there is contradictory testimony as to exactly what happened there."[242] So, while some traditions might suggest that Gehenna was the entrance to the underworld, Biblical exegesis

---

[241] Jeremiah 7:33
[242] Fudge, The Fire That Consumes 161

suggests that the fulfilment must still be in keeping with Isaiah's description. In other words, it must be a judgment of destruction, because the original context described dead bodies being eaten by maggots.[243] The emphasis was on destruction and not on any sense of some form of continuous existence. The idea that *gehenna* was a place of destruction is also supported by other teaching such as in Matthew 10:28, where it says that the soul and body would be destroyed.

Therefore, the Hebrew understanding of *gehenna* as a real place that prophetically described total rejection and loss without future hope cannot be ignored. Regardless of whether *gehenna* was used to describe judgment in this life or the afterlife, the outcome for those subject to *gehenna* was their destruction.

In other passages of the New Testament, destruction was a recurrent theme. Paul says that it was not the custom of the Romans to deliver any man to destruction, before the accused meets the accusers.[244] In James 4:12 it says, "There is only one lawgiver and Judge, the One who is able to save and to destroy."[245] The word destroy (*apollumi*), is the same word translated "perish" or "die" in John 3:16. In that case, the middle voice had a reflexive meaning, where the

---

[243] While there might be some disagreement over traditional views as to whether a rubbish dump existed in Gehenna, historical acts of Judgment described by Jeremiah, where bodies were left to rot suggest that it was possible.
[244] Acts 25:15
[245] James 4:12 (NASB)

subject was responsible for the action described by the verb; they perished because they chose not to believe. However, James used destroy in the future active infinitive, where the subject is the agent of an action which impacts on others. In whatever form the verb was used, it means utter and complete destruction.

In Luke 13, Jesus noted the deaths of two groups of people. One was through the actions of the authorities and the other possibly through an accident. In both cases, Jesus pointed out that repentance was required to avoid the same fate - *apollumi*, which was death or destruction. The question was raised whether these people deserved to die, which is something Jesus denied. Yet he used the accounts of the tragedies to indicate that death is a consequence of unrepentance for all. Jesus did not mention the fate of the wicked here in reference or thought to any future existence. His point was that unless you repent, you will end up like these people, dead or destroyed. Conversely, repentance brings life.

This is why Peter could say that the Lord was not willing that any should perish or be destroyed (*apollumi*), but that all should come to repentance.[246] Here, perish is in the middle voice and is a reflexive action. Man is destroyed because he is unrepentant and has brought destruction on himself.

While Scripture states that all men will be

---

[246] 2 Peter 3:9 (NKJV)

114

resurrected, only the righteous will receive immortality. The resurrection for those who have done good is a resurrection of *zoe* life.[247] This is the great hope in which we have confidence and follows the pattern of Christ who went before us, who died and was raised back to life.

Job who was facing death predicted the possibility of living once again when he said, "Even after my skin has been destroyed, in my flesh I will see God."[248] The miracle is the intervention of God to restore the *psuche* life that was dead and buried in the grave back to *zoe* life. However, for those who have done evil it is a resurrection of condemnation,[249] which must have an entirely different purpose. Paul's teaching was that the resurrection to life brings immortality and immunity from death or corruption. Therefore, the resurrection of condemnation suggests that the wicked will not receive immortality, and are not immune to further death.

If these ideas are true, then Scripture should clearly explain that the wicked would rise in the resurrection, but eventually cease to exist. Revelation 20:6 described the first resurrection as the resurrection of life for the *just* over which the second death had no

---

[247] John 5:28-29
[248] Job 19:25-26 (NCV)
[249] John 5:29

power.[250] A few verses later in Revelation 20:12, it described another resurrection - the resurrection of the *unjust*.[251] This resurrection was for the rest of the dead or the dead that remained after the resurrection of the just. Their final destination was the lake of fire, which was described as the second death.[252]

Therefore, while the first resurrection described the just as *souls* standing before the throne of God, the resurrection of the unjust merely stated that the *dead* were judged, and cast into the lake of fire. The unjust are referred to in their resurrection as the dead, whereas the just are referred to as souls. As we have seen, a soul is a self-existent being. This is useful, because these souls are receiving their reward, which is life. The dead however only face a second death.

The fact that the unjust are resurrected dead, confirms our understanding that life is only given to those who do good. Of course, these dead are presumably somehow alive or at least conscious during the judgment proceedings. However, we can only speculate on the nature of this type of intermediate period of existence. It might be possible to argue that

---

[250] While the first resurrection appears to be for the martyrs and those who did not worship the beast, it cannot be an exclusive event as suggested by verse 6, which states that those who have *part in the first resurrection* are blessed.

[251] The word resurrection is not actually used in this verse, but it is reasonable to assume that this is the Resurrection of Condemnation referred to in John 5:29, and therefore must be the second resurrection, as implied by the description of the first resurrection in Revelation 20:6

[252] It is important to note that there is no mention of eternal torment or punishment. This idea will be discussed further on.

they are in fact dead without conscious existence, but that would seem to undermine the emphasis on the resurrection of condemnation, which is for the purposes of passing judgment.

Whatever the metaphysical state of the wicked dead in their resurrection, they are certainly not the possessors of a new imperishable body. The incorruptible nature of the resurrection body of the just means that the resurrection of the unjust has to be different. Because their final destination is the second death, it suggests that they are not immortal or incorruptible.

In addition, the idea of the second death is contrasted by the souls in the first resurrection, who are blessed because the second death has no power over them. It has no power over them because the resurrection to life has granted immortality, which is immunity from death. However, the 'wicked dead' appear briefly for the purposes of condemnation, before disappearing into the lake of fire. The lake of fire signifies the complete and utter loss of the unjust to that point or place in time, where there is no possibility of return to existence.

These are ideas that for some may be difficult to accept, given that the consensus of the Church has been that the unjust would continue to experience some form of existence throughout eternity. While the Church has made valuable contributions to the development of theological ideas, this does not mean that every doctrine is valid. Jesus' complaint to the Jews was that they worshipped in vain, because they taught as doctrine the commands of man.[253] If the doctrine of the immortality of the soul was closer in idea to Greek philosophy than orthodox Hebrew beliefs about the nature of man and judgment, then the implications for interpretation need to be fully understood.

While sound doctrine is essential to the Christian Faith, there is always the possibility that some beliefs may not accurately reflect the Biblical emphasis. When ideas become widely accepted, it becomes very difficult to accept the possibility that those ideas may differ from the message that should have been passed on. This is why comparing scripture with scripture is so important in defining essential beliefs. When we consider how the Church has defined certain ideas, it is important to consider the possibility that those ideas do not really agree with a scriptural emphasis.

If we consider the beliefs of the early Church, there is evidence to suggest the possibility that a shift of emphasis occurred at some stages in the development of theological ideas. For example, in the 2nd Century, the apostolic Fathers seemed content with biblical words and phrases. "They did not elaborate on them – or eliminate them."[254] We could suggest that there did not seem to be any need for them to go

---

[253] Matthew 15:9
[254] Fudge, The Fire that Consumes, 361

beyond the obvious meanings - although some might debate what those were. However, by the beginning of the third century, there seems to have been a change. Tertullian had embraced everlasting torment and Origen looked to universal restoration. Tertullian and Origen based "their views on the philosophical doctrine that all souls are immortal, though both concede that God created them and could (but will not) destroy them as well."[255] In this case, we would have to consider how Greek philosophy might have influenced the development of theological ideas.

These ideas then raise questions about Hell, which has often been described as a place of eternal torment and punishment in eternal fire, for those that do not accept salvation through Jesus Christ. This eternal torment is a never-ending punishment, where the unbeliever is cast into hell to burn forever, suffering continuously in anguish as they gnash their teeth. This view of Hell has generally been the traditional view, and the view that has been held by most, but not all Christians.

In addition, some hold strongly to this traditional view because it is believed that Jesus spoke extensively about Hell and about those who would be tormented. However, Hell is an English word that was assigned to various Greek and Hebrew words by some English translations. Understanding this issue is very

---

[255] Fudge, The Fire that Consumes, 361

important, because certain connotations that have been generated by general usage are likely to have controverted the writers intended purpose. This confusion is likely to become more significant as the mythology of hell continues to become popularised, and retold to the masses through the medium of film and television.

The words affected in this way were *gehenna, hades and sheol. Sheol* and *hades* were the Hebrew and Greek equivalent for the grave, and *gehenna* referred to a valley outside Jerusalem with strong historical and symbolic connotations. Each of these words had different meanings, best understood within the relevant textual and historical contexts, while taking into account the way they were used by Jesus and the New Testament writers.

### *Everlasting Torment in the Gospels*

In Matthew Chapter 23, Jesus passed judgment on the Pharisees with a number of woes, in which he rebuked them for their hypocrisy and lawlessness. He clearly stated that they were also guilty by association for past acts of persecution and unrighteousness, and therefore responsible for all the blood shed by the prophets from Able to Zechariah. In addition, they would persecute the future prophets to come, which would only serve to further justify and fulfil Jesus' warning of impending doom. Consequently, their actions would "bring upon them all the righteous blood shed on the Earth," and that they would not escape the condemnation (*krisis*) of hell (*gehenna*).[256]

Because the word condemnation mentioned in verse 33 is *krisis*, which denotes a passing of judgment upon a person or thing, Jesus was clearly condemning the current generation to a coming judgment. He also clearly specifies that generation's contribution to the events for which they would be judged.

The condemnation of *gehenna* then becomes symbolic of a future judgment. It becomes a prophetic statement of the future fate of a people who had rejected God and followed lawlessness. There was no sense in Jesus' teaching that those subject to the condemnation of *gehenna* would suffer eternal torment. Because Jeremiah described *gehenna* as a place of destruction, this suggests that Jesus had in mind the same form of Judgment. Therefore, the religious and political leadership of the day were indignant, because Jesus claimed that they were the subjects of specific prophecy on whom judgment would fall.

The links between the place *gehenna*, the symbolism, and the possibility of a real future event, was suggested by a prophetic statement by Jesus made against Jerusalem. "The days will come upon you,

---

[256] Matthew 23:33

when your enemies will set up ramparts around you and surround you, and hem you in on every side. They will crush you to the ground, you and your children within you, and they will not leave within you one stone upon another; because you did not recognize the time of your visitation from God."[257]

The combination of the warning of the condemnation of *gehenna*, and this prophetic statement, suggests a specific event in history. In addition, this particular teaching could not be for some future generation or some after life event, because these warnings were specific to those to whom the warnings were made. As he pointed out in Matthew 23:33; the religious leaders were a bunch of serpents, a brood of vipers; they would not escape the condemnation of *gehenna*.

To summarise Jesus' teaching,[258] he often taught about the unprofitable, lazy and ill prepared servants who would be cast into the outer darkness, and where there would be weeping and gnashing of teeth. The parables described the impending doom of a people who had failed to use what they had been given, and that what they had was about to be taken away from them - or that they were to lose certain privileges.

The outcome would be that the sons of the Kingdom would be cast into outer darkness, and others

---

[257] Luke 19:43-44 (NRSV)
[258] For example Matthew 24-25

would receive their inheritance.[259] These ideas were persistent themes in Jesus' teaching. In the parables of the talents, misuse of opportunity led to total ruin and loss. The lazy servant lost everything he had and what he had was given to others.[260] Jesus talked about the foolish virgins who were not ready for the Bride Groom, and were shut out of the wedding festivities.[261] Likewise, the man who was not dressed for the wedding was cast out into the outer darkness.[262]

The language of outer darkness does not fit the common view of a fiery hell. However, this phrase does support the prophetic condemnation of a sinful generation. It signals the loss of nationhood, religious identity, and covenant relationship with God, an idea that was brought out in Jesus' use of the Wedding parables.[263]

It is the implications of what he said that ultimately led to the crucifixion of Christ. The rejection of the King and the Kingdom of God leading to ruin and loss for the religious leaders of the day, can be no more clearly stated than in the parable of the landowner.[264] In this parable, a certain landowner planted a vineyard, leased it to vinedressers, and then went off into a far country. At harvest time, he sent his

---

[259] Matthew 8:12 (NKJV)
[260] Matthew 25:21-29
[261] Matthew 25.2
[262] Matthew 22:11-14
[263] Mark 2:19
[264] Matthew 21:33

servants to the vinedressers, that he might receive its fruit, but the vinedressers beat and killed the servants. Eventually the landowner sent his son who was also killed.

Jesus then asked the religious leaders what they thought would happen to the vinedressers. They replied that the landowner would come and destroy them. Jesus then quoted Scripture that the rejected building stone would become the chief cornerstone, and linked this event with the Kingdom of God being taken away and given to another. He goes on to say, "The one who falls on this stone will be broken to pieces; and it will crush anyone on whom it falls."[265]

At this point, the Chief Priests and Pharisees perceived that he was speaking about them. Whether or not they fully understood the implications of what Jesus had said, they were certainly offended. They would have sought to have Jesus arrested had it not been for the support of the crowds. However, the message from Jesus is clear. They had rejected the chief cornerstone; the stone would fall on them; they would be destroyed. The point to all this teaching is that they would not escape the condemnation or judgment of *gehenna*. However, *gehenna* translated by the word hell tends to create a different type of understanding about this judgment, especially if extra Biblical mythology forms the basis of interpretation. We have already seen

---

[265] Matthew 21:44 (NRSV)

how *gehenna* referred to an actual place, with strong symbolic connotations of destruction, without reference to some future state of existence.

It is important to note the sense of urgency in these warnings. Jesus was calling the nation to righteousness, and he expected those listening to him to get right with God before it was too late. For example, Jesus stated that it was better to cut off an offending body part to avoid sin, than to have the whole body cast into *gehenna*.[266] Jesus had used a well-known physical location with traditional and symbolic relevance to make a striking overstatement. Jesus would not really expect people to cut off their hands. Using a form of sarcasm, he urged the people to repent from wickedness before it was too late.

Stories like that in Matthew 5:25-26 also suggested this expectancy. "If your enemy is taking you to court, become friends quickly, before you go to court. Otherwise, your enemy might turn you over to the judge, and the judge might give you to a guard to put you in jail. I tell you the truth; you will not leave there until you have paid everything you owe."[267] The fact that the one in prison might possibly get out if he pays all his pennies, suggests that this passage does not represent an afterlife experience. It is a call to righteousness in light of the coming judgment of Israel.

---

[266] Matthew 5:30
[267] Matthew 5:25-26 (NCV)

The possibility that this judgment of *gehenna* would soon befall the nation of Israel, was also prophetically stated through Malachi who says, "I will send you Elijah the prophet before that great and terrifying day of the Lord's judging."[268] Because Jesus had declared that this Elijah was in fact John the Baptist,[269] the event referred to by Malachi would now soon occur. Therefore, this Day of Judgment was going to fall on the generation to whom the message of judgment was given.

In addition, John the Baptist himself suggested the possibility of a judgment, when he responded to the Pharisees and Sadducees who had come to his baptism. With rhetorical cynicism he states, "Who warned you to flee from the *wrath to come*?"[270] Because John went on to say that the axe was already laid to the root of the tree, the text suggests that the word *come* means *about to be*. Therefore it was the 'coming wrath of God' that was already in progress when John spoke, and that "every tree that does not produce good fruit will be chopped down and thrown into the fire."[271] Malachi described this judgment as the great and awesome[272] day of the Lord, in which "he will turn the hearts of fathers to their children and the hearts of children to

---

[268] Malachi 4:5 (NCV)
[269] Matthew 11:14
[270] Matthew 3:7 (NKJV)
[271] Matthew 3:10 (NLT)
[272] Awesome here means terrible or dreadful. The NCV translates this as the "great and terrifying day of the Lord's judging."

their fathers, lest I come and strike the land with a decree of utter destruction."[273] These warnings of imminent judgment suggest that it was likely that the condemnation of *gehenna* had its historical fulfillment. Because the considered period for a generation was about 40 years, it is likely that this judgment probably referred to the Destruction of Jerusalem in 70 AD.

On the 10th August 70 AD, the temple was burned and levelled to the ground by the Romans following a long siege. The historian Josephus claimed that over a million people were killed, and therefore the disposal of the dead would have been a significant problem. This suggests that the bodies would have been dumped and burned, and the condemnation of *gehenna* would have been fulfilled, as recorded by Josephus...

*Now the seditious at first gave orders that the dead should be buried out of the public treasury, as not enduring the stench of their dead bodies. But afterwards, when they could not do that, they had them cast down from the walls into the valleys beneath. (War 5.12.3).*

While these events may seem a little harsh, they were not unusual in the context of Israel's history. The fact that the prophecies of the destruction of the temple in 70 AD were so accurately fulfilled within a

---

[273] Malachi 4:6 (ESV)

generation, reminds us that God is in control. These events also serve to remind us of the severity of God towards sin. Whatever ways the character and nature of God's judgments might be understood, the events occurred because Israel did not heed the warnings. If Israel had repented and acted in obedience, then the outcome might have been different. Understanding how these passages might apply to historical events makes it difficult to assign them to an afterlife punishment. As in the Old Testament warnings by prophets of old, the emphasis was on obtaining life and avoiding judgment leading to death.

It is important to note that the quote from Isaiah 66:24, which is often used to justify the traditional view of hell, actually described how the people would go out to see the dead bodies of those who had rebelled against God. This suggests that Israel had once again suffered the very fate, which was so clearly prophesized by Isaiah and again by Jesus. These ideas suggest that *gehenna* was a real place, prophetically descriptive of historical judgments in which the dead were destroyed; which means that such references cannot be used to support the view of hell as a place of everlasting torment.

Other references regarding judgment made by Jesus cannot be used to build a doctrine of hell, because they are unclear about the state of the future circumstances of those being judged or they do not support the traditional view of Hell.

For example, Jesus says, "On the last day many people will say to me, 'Lord, Lord, we spoke for you, and through you we forced out demons and did many miracles.' Then I will tell them clearly, 'Get away from me, you who do evil. I never knew you.'"[274] In this passage, it only says that these people were rejected. It does not say what happens to them. Likewise, in Matthew 16:26, the only real conclusion that can be made is that man loses his life when he attempts to gain the world. There is nothing about a future unpleasant state of existence. In Mark 3:27-29 it says that the one that blasphemes against the Holy Spirit is subject to eternal condemnation. This does not mean there will be continuous punishment, but rather that the judgment made will stand forever.

After examining Jesus' teachings where there is reference to historical judgment, or the words *gehenna* or *hades* were used, there are only about three references from the Gospels that are of interest. Even then, these references cannot be used to support a traditional view of Hell as a place of never ending torment, because there are reasonable explanations for each. Two of these passages are similar; The Parables of the dragnet,[275] and the parables of the tares or weeds,[276] described judgment with identical results.

In both cases the good and the bad fish and

---

[274] Matthew 7:21-23 (NCV)
[275] Matthew 13:47-50
[276] Matthew 13:39-42

plants are left together until a time of judgment. Then they are collected up, sorted, and the bad fish or plants are cast into the furnace of fire. While Jesus says there will be wailing and gnashing of teeth, there is no indication that this means that the wicked are suffering forever in torment. In the Greek text, there was no conjunction between the casting into the fire and the wailing and gnashing of teeth. Therefore, it is unclear when this wailing and gnashing occurs, and how long it lasts. If the unrighteous were to suffer in eternal torment, the text should clearly say, "Cast them into the furnace of fire, *where there will be never ending* wailing and gnashing of teeth."

In addition, we would also probably expect the text to mention some further details about the suffering. However, the 'wailing and gnashing of teeth' is likely to be an idiomatic expression of regret that describes the reaction to the judgment. It is possible that these passages could refer to the final judgment leading to the Second Death, in which case such a reaction would be entirely credible. The resurrection of condemnation was for the purposes of giving an account, where those whose names were not found in the Book of Life were cast into the lake of fire, which was called the Second Death.[277] Those experiencing this judgment might certainly have shown some form of regret at the knowledge of their certain demise.

---

[277] Revelation 20:11-15

This argument could simply stand by itself, but it is possible that these passages also refer to the Judgment of Israel. The reason for this is that the parables referred to the end of the age (*aion*) and not the end of the world (*kosmos*). The word *aion* can be translated either as *age* or *ever* depending on context. When used as age it "generally referred to the present era, as opposed to the future age."[278] It also described a period marked by certain spiritual and moral characteristics.[279]

The disciples who had been listening to Jesus obviously expected that certain things would happen within a marked period of time. This is because in the beginning of Matthew 24, they asked him what would be the signs of the end of the age and of his return. Jesus responded with a detailed prophetic description of events, which they themselves would personally experience, and for which they must be prepared.

However, the obvious difficulty with this is that Jesus also seemed to time his return with the end of the age - and the fulfilment of certain events during which at least some of his disciples would live to experience.

While theologians propose a number of solutions to this problem,[280] this does not affect our

---

[278] Youngblood, R. F., Bruce, F. F., Harrison, R. K., & Thomas Nelson Publishers. Bible dictionary.; Includes index. Nashville: T. Nelson. (1995). *Nelson's new illustrated Bible dictionary*. Rev. ed. of: Nelson's illustrated
[279] Vine, W. E., Unger, M. F., & White, W. (1996).
[280] For example: One view is that the writer included eschatological and non-eschatological material to answer the disciple's two different questions.

basic premise. One cannot read Matthew 24, and ignore the sense of urgency in Jesus' response and the relevant nature of these events for his disciples. For example, Jesus warned them that when the *abomination of desolation* stood in the Holy Place, then those in Judea were to flee to the Mountains.[281] They were not to take anything with them or go back into the fields to get their clothes; and they were to pray that these things would not happen on the Sabbath. These statements placed the events of Jesus' warning into a contemporary Jewish context familiar to his disciples.

In other passages of Scripture, Jesus told his disciples that they would be persecuted, betrayed and put to death.[282] He also exhorted them to be alert at all times, and that they would have the strength to escape all these things.[283] It is significant that these warnings were made in the context of the destruction of Jerusalem,[284] which Jesus expected to occur within the lifetime of the Disciples.[285]

These ideas suggest that it would be necessary for them to recognise the elements of the various prophetic references, which were a personal warning

Therefore, we can discern between those things that have already happened-the destruction of the temple and those things yet to be fulfilled-Christ's return. The Preterist view would argue that all or most of these things were fulfilled by AD 70. This would include the return or appearance of Jesus as a 'parousia' of Judgment for Israel and not as an end of the world event.
[281] Matthew 24:15-16
[282] Luke 21:12-16
[283] Luke 21:36
[284] Luke 21:20 (NKJV)
[285] Matthew 23:36

requiring preparation and watchfulness.

Therefore, the imagery of these parables might suggest a transitional period for the Church and Israel, which would co-exist side by side until a time of sifting. This transitional phase existed, because God could not judge one until the other was firmly established. This is an idea supported by John the Baptist's statement that the "winnowing fork is in his hand, and he will clear his threshing floor and will gather his wheat into the granary; but the chaff he will burn with unquenchable fire."[286]

It was evident that this 'sifting' would occur within the current generation, because John seemed to suggest that the Pharisees and Sadducees were part of the 'tree' to which the axe was already laid.[287] Therefore, it is possible that these references focus on the act of judgment as a specific act at a point and time in history.

The third reference is in Matthew 25:44-46. It says that the wicked will go into everlasting punishment, but the righteous into eternal life. However, an everlasting punishment does not necessarily mean an everlasting continuous act or series of punishments. It can simply mean a punishment, which has an everlasting effect. When Adam and Eve sinned, their punishment was death, described as the

---

[286] Matthew 3:12 (NRSV)
[287] Matthew 3:10

dissolution of their bodies back to the elements from which they were formed. It is that absolute place or point in time, when any opportunity for life or existence has been forever completely and utterly lost. This is made apparent by the other part of this verse, which states that eternal life awaits the righteous. The parallelism of ideas reinforces the authors intended meaning that the punishment being talked about is a death, which is everlasting. If everlasting life is the hope, then the antithesis can only be everlasting death.

This passage also states that the destination of the wicked is the eternal fire,[288] which is synonymous with the lake of fire in Revelation, which is called the second death.[289] This second death does not describe the wicked suffering in eternal torment. Fire in the Bible was symbolic of destruction and those subject to the eternal fire (the second death) are ultimately destroyed.

These ideas do not stand by themselves. Scripture stated that Jesus came to abolish death and grant immortality. Immortality was immunity from death, and therefore the second death is an eternal punishment, because that immunity is lost forever. Considering all these issues, it becomes difficult to be dogmatic about the possibility that Jesus thought that the wicked would suffer forever in agony. Many of the passages are idiomatic and prophetic warnings, many

---

[288] Matthew 25:41
[289] Revelation 20:14

of which were clearly destined for the current generation. Some passages obviously referred to a judgment beyond this life, but there was no clear, consistent and explicit teaching in the Gospels, which suggested the eternal torment of the wicked.

### *Everlasting Torment in Revelation*

In the Book of Revelation, it stated that those who worshipped the beast and his image were tormented with fire and brimstone in the presence of the holy angels, and in the presence of the Lamb.[290] The smoke of their torment ascends forever and ever and they have no rest day or night, who worship the beast and his image, and whoever receives the mark of his name. This at first might appear to be a very clear description of everlasting torment in the afterlife for the wicked. However, there are a number of problems and issues that are not immediately apparent.

Firstly, Revelation was written to describe certain events, which would soon take place after the prophecies were given. Prophecy aims to have immediate benefit to the intended audience. It encourages, exhorts, and warns struggling Christians in a time of great persecution, explaining that God is in control and explicitly declaring that evil will ultimately

---

[290] Revelation 14:8-11

fail. Therefore, the Christians reading Revelation should have been able to identify elements of prophecy with their own real world experiences. This can be stated with confidence, because Jesus specifically stated that these things would soon take place.[291]

Because there was a sense of urgency in Revelation, it indicates that something significant and dramatic was going to occur. It is possible that the events depicted are metaphorical and symbolic accounts of the strange and various events leading up to the destruction of Jerusalem.

The next problem is that those being tormented are only those who worshipped the beast. It must be possible that Christians, for whom this revelation was given about events that would soon take place, would have been able to identify this beast. John's use of a puzzle called a gematria, in which numbers were used to represent certain letters, supports this idea.[292] Using the numerical values of the Hebrew letters in זרונ רסק (*Nron Qsr-Nero Caesar*) allows the reader to arrive at the number "666."[293] This particular code identifies to John's contemporaries a real life person whom they would know about, but for obvious reasons could not specifically name.

Besides this, there are a number of scriptures

---

[291] Revelation 1:1 (NLT)
[292] http://en.wikipedia.org/wiki/Number_of_the_beast
[293] Revelation 13:18  Some Manuscripts use the number 616 calculated from *Nro Qsr*

that align with the historical events of the time. For example, "five kings have already fallen, the sixth now reigns, and the seventh is yet to come, but his reign will be brief."[294] These kings probably referred to certain Roman Emperors that Christians would have been able to recognise. The historian Josephus listed the emperors as Julius, Augustus, Tiberius, Caligula, and Claudius who were the five kings who had fallen. At the time of John's Revelation, there was Nero and then after him came Galba.[295] In addition to this, it says that the "beast was allowed to wage war against God's holy people and to conquer them."[296] It was likely that this referred to Nero, because Revelation 13:5 says that the beast would continue for 42 months. Nero's persecution of Christians started in 64 AD and lasted until his death in June 68 AD, which was three and a half years, or 42 months.[297]

The next problem with this passage of Scripture is that those who worshipped the beast were tormented with fire and brimstone in the presence of God. It is logical that this could not be an eternal event. While it says that the smoke of their torment ascends forever and ever, this is likely to be a metaphorical way of saying that the memory of this event will last forever, but not the event itself. Hyperbole is used to underline

---

[294] Revelation 17:10 (NLT)
[295] http://en.wikipedia.org/wiki/The_Beast_(preterism)
[296] Revelation 13:7 (NLT)
[297] http://en.wikipedia.org/wiki/The_Beast_(preterism)

the severity of the circumstances. This is a bit like saying the preacher went on forever and ever.

Because of numerous supporting scriptures that suggest that eternal torment is not the uniform and consistent witness of Scripture, it is reasonable to assume that this passage is symbolic, but refers to real events. Therefore, this passage might describe certain events during the period of persecution, leading up to and including the siege of Jerusalem prior to the destruction of the temple in 70 AD.

### Everlasting Torment in the Epistles

These ideas also need to be understood in the context of the views of the other New Testament writers. In the Epistles, no one mentioned eternal torment as a punishment in the afterlife. Paul never once mentioned eternal torment in hell as a consequence for the wicked, because he believed that the wages of sin was death.[298] A simple search of the original Greek words also tells us that Paul never used *gehenna*,[299] and he only used *hades* once, which is usually translated as grave or death.[300]

This means that Paul never once made any effort

---

[298] Romans 6:23
[299] The only other occurrence of *gehenna* is in James 3:6 but only in reference to the work of the tongue.
[300] 1 Corinthians 15:55

to describe anything that sounds or looks remotely like the hell popularized by the traditional view. If hell as an everlasting torment of unbelievers were true, then there should have been some form of teaching from Paul on the subject.

By contrast, Paul's use of other words to explain existential issues is significant. For example, he used the word death about 47 times, but there was no indication that Paul thought that man naturally survived death. In Paul's mind, death was the enemy that would be defeated and from which God would rescue man.[301] He also frequently described death as the punishment for sin.[302] In like manner, he also used the word perish[303] or destruction[304] about 12 times to describe the outcome for those that were not being saved. Altogether, about 30 verses make clear references to death or destruction being the outcome for sin, without any suggestion of some form of continuous existence for the wicked. For example, Paul stated that God had endured with patience the objects of wrath made for destruction.[305]

The interdependent themes of sin, death, and life are exemplified in Romans 6. Paul stated that we had been united with Christ in his death through baptism.

---

[301] Rom 6:4, 6:5, 1 Cor 15:26, 15:54, 15:55, 2 Cor 1:10, 2 Tim 1:10
[302] Rom 1:32, 5:12, 5:14, 5:17, 5:21, 6:16, 6:23, 7:5, 7:10, 7:24, 8:6, 1 Cor 15:21, 2 Cor 7:10
[303] Rom 2:12, 1 Cor 10:9, 1 Cor 10:10, 2 Cor 2:15, 2 Cor 4:3, 2 Thess 2:10
[304] Rom 9:22, Phil 1:28, 3:19, 1 Tim 6:9, 1 Thess 5:3, 2 Thess 1:9
[305] Romans 9:22

Because of this, our sinful natures were crucified with Christ, so that sin might lose its power. The proof was the resurrection of Christ, who rose from the dead never to die again. The death he died, he died to sin, which meant that the believer should consider themselves dead to sin and alive to God in Christ Jesus.[306]

Paul goes on to describe how the choice to obey God leads to righteousness, holiness and eternal life. However, the old way of life was a slavery to sin that led to death.[307] "Do you not know that if you present yourselves to anyone as obedient slaves, you are slaves of the one whom you obey, either of sin, which leads to death, or of obedience, which leads to righteousness?[308] According to Paul, our sinful passions were aroused by the law, which produced the fruit leading to death. This death must be physical death, because these ideas were illustrated through Adam's disobedience, whose actions led to death for all.[309]

The solution to the problem of sin and death was repentance, but there was no indication that sin would lead to eternal torment, because worldly sorrow only produced death.[310] Therefore, there were two choices offered by Paul - obedience and repentance leading to

---

[306] Romans 6:5-11
[307] Romans 6:16-23
[308] Romans 6:16 (NRSV)
[309] Romans 5:12
[310] 2 Corinthians 7:10

life, or sin leading to death. While Paul notes that the impenitent were storing up wrath for the day of God's righteous judgment, and that there would be anguish and distress for everyone who did evil,[311] it was clear that this wrath led to the destruction of those being judged.[312] "Their end is destruction; their god is the belly; and their glory is in their shame; their minds are set on earthly things."[313]

Although the believer enjoyed a new life in Christ, he remained subject to a physical death. However, Paul taught that when the end comes, Christ will turn over the Kingdom to God the Father, and then the last enemy death would be destroyed. As we have already seen, Paul makes the link between the resurrection of our perishable earthly bodies, their transformation into heavenly bodies that will never die, and the defeat of death.[314]

> *"Death has been swallowed up in victory."*
> *"Where, O death, is your victory?*
> *Where, O death, is your sting?"*[315]

In 1 Corinthians 15:18, Paul defending the resurrection wrote that if there is no resurrection of the dead, Christ had not risen and those that had already

---

[311] Romans 2:5-9
[312] Romans 2:12
[313] Philippians 3:19 (NRSV)
[314] 1 Corinthians 15:50-54
[315] 1 Corinthians 15:54-55

died had perished. As already stated previously, the word perished can be translated as destroyed. In other words, if there is no resurrection, then those who had already died had been destroyed. Paul's teaching would only make sense if man was mortal and perish meant destruction. Alternatively, if perish meant eternal torment, then the *just* would have to be punished, which would be contradictory to the promises of God.

Of course, it would not make sense that the just would suffer because there was no resurrection. However, because perish is likely to mean destruction or death, the resurrection would be their only hope. Logically, if there is a resurrection, then the just are not destroyed, while this fate would have to remain for the unjust.

Other Epistles follow similar themes. In Hebrews 10:39, it says that those who shrink back are destroyed (*apoleia*). Interestingly, various translations tackle this verse in different ways. The King James Version translates the word as perdition, while the New Revised Standard Version uses the word lost. The word means total destruction and it is important to note there was no mention of sinners suffering in eternal torment.

Peter also used the same word to describe destruction for the wicked. "But by the same word the present heavens and earth have been reserved for fire, being kept until the Day of Judgment and destruction of the godless."[316] It would be unreasonable to assume that this destruction described eternal torment in hell.

The idea that a punishment of destruction does not actually destroy is a contradiction. This destruction will be utter and complete, because the whole self will be lost forever with no chance of return. The death of man leading to the dissolution of the body was the first death, from which God resurrects both the righteous and the wicked - the righteous to immortality and the wicked to condemnation. This condemnation leads to total loss of existence in the lake of fire (the second death). Therefore, Jesus' words to fear Him who can destroy both body and soul are fulfilled. The nature of this destruction under the wrath of God will introduce an unavoidable reality, from which there is no chance of return.

To build a doctrine of everlasting torment requires many assumptions. We would have to incorrectly accept the word hell as a translation for *gehenna*.[317] We would also have to disregard the fact that while the use of attached references to Isaiah suggests that the fire is not quenched, the bodies are actually dead. We would have to overlook the confusion often made between *Hades* and Hell, and how some translations use Hell instead of *Hades* or *Gehenna*. We would have to ignore the Biblical

---

[316] 2 Peter 3:7 (NRSV)
[317] This objection relates to the idea that hell means many things that *gehenna* did not.

understanding of *Hades,* which like the *Sheol* of the Old Testament was the grave. We would also have to overlook the hope of rescue back from the grave to life that was central to Hebrew thinking.

We would have to ignore the fact that there was no suggestion that the grave was a permanent place of torment or that there was any form of conscious existence. In addition, we would have to ignore the fact that while *Hades* is thrown into the lake of fire and destroyed in the last judgment, before this happens it is first emptied of its dead.

We would have to overlook the possibility that references that use certain phrases, such as 'being cast into the outer darkness', could actually apply to judgment events that have already occurred. Finally, we would have to discount the possibility that Eternal Punishment can mean a punishment that stands forever, as opposed to meaning punishments that continue forever. However, Scripture consistently and clearly describes the outcome for man's disobedience as death, and whose only remedy is God's provision of life in the resurrection.

# Resurrection in the Acts of the Apostles

Paul was very careful in providing a detailed explanation of the process that transforms us for eternal life, which is the physical resurrection into new and spiritually modified bodies. If the resurrection of the body is essential for the future existence of man, then this idea should be emphasised throughout Scripture. The antithesis of this idea is the possibility of a soul surviving death without the body.

The disciple's reaction to the death of Jesus makes an important contribution to an understanding of these issues. For example, they did not express the hope that he was not dead. They did not pretend that he had gone to a better place, or that he was safe in God's hands. These thoughts might have been the response of those that believed that death was a mere transition to another level of existence. However, their response revealed the general human response to the loss of a loved one; they were devastated and struck with grief. It epitomised the general Hebrew understanding that the only hope for man was the resurrection in the eschatological fulfilment of God's purposes. Therefore, the Disciples' hope that Jesus was going to redeem Israel[318] was completely lost, because Jesus' death was seen and understood as being the complete end of the man.

Understanding the nature of the death of Christ is essential. If we believe that man was naturally immortal and incapable of death, then when Jesus had died, he must have somehow continued to live on. However, how could Jesus have fully tasted death if in fact he continued to exist after the death of his body? The whole point about the cross is that Jesus died and death is the end of existence. You cannot say that something dies if in fact something about it continues to exist in some form. Therefore....."we must affirm that Jesus died, and in doing so we must feel the full theological weight of death...that death is both relationlessness and inactivity..."[319]

Because Jesus did not stay dead, the narratives that described the resurrection should help to explain something about the relationship between life, death and the body for the believer. These points cannot be ignored, because the physical resurrection from the dead makes Christianity unique. The survival of the soul after death is however contradictory to the purpose of the resurrection, where death was defeated through the power of God who raised people back to life.

---

[318] Luke 24:21
[319] Wright, Churchman 122/2 (Church Society) 110

In addition, the disparate difference in the Disciples' understanding of Jesus' death, before and after the resurrection, revealed an important shift in the understanding of the events they had now experienced. For example, before his resurrection they struggled to make sense of what Jesus was saying.[320] Afterwards, they boldly and clearly asserted that Jesus was the Messiah, and God had proved this by raising him from the dead. It was very unlikely that the disciples would have gone around saying that their leader had risen from the grave, unless this had actually happened. Therefore, only a real event could account for the radical enthusiasm of the Disciples. More importantly though, as Tom Wright notes, "when the early Christians said that Jesus had risen from the dead they knew that they were saying that something had happened to him, which had happened to nobody else and which nobody had expected to happen."[321]

In addition to these ideas, Jesus' resurrection body, while being the same was in some way different. He could eat, talk, and touch and yet he seemed to be able to appear suddenly in locked rooms.[322] Jesus, the first fruits of the resurrection, having been further clothed had defeated death. Therefore, the way in which the Disciples explained the death and resurrection of Christ will help contribute to an

---

[320] John 16:17
[321] Tom Wright, Surprised by Hope, (SPCK, 2007) 48
[322] John 20:19

understanding of the key elements of the Christian Faith. This is because the preservation of important content will become evident through the presentation of the message. The key themes will also help to explain the nature of man, life, death and the judgment. In particular, the way in which the early Christians responded to Jesus' command to preach the Gospel in the Acts of the Apostles should be useful in helping to clarify these issues.

After the ascension of Christ, the Disciples were gathered together during the time of the Festival of Pentecost.[323] As they met, the Holy Spirit came in power on the disciples and they began speaking in other tongues. A crowd of devout Jews from different nations, who had gathered in Jerusalem for the festivities, were intrigued that the Disciples were able to speak in their own languages and sought for an explanation.

Peter began preaching and quoting from the Old Testament,[324] with the intention of making the point that Jesus of Nazareth was no ordinary man. According to the definite plan and foreknowledge of God, Jesus had been crucified, but then God had raised him up, freeing him from death because it was impossible for him to be held in its power.[325]

Peter was keen to emphasise that Jesus had

---

[323] Acts 2
[324] Acts 2:17
[325] Acts 2:24 (NRSV)

148

defeated the power of death, and had come back from a place of being dead. He also went on to make the point that the prophecies, which he used to support the resurrection of Christ as the messiah, could not apply to King David, because David was still dead in his tomb.[326] This argument is an important contribution to Peter's case for the resurrection of Jesus. This is because Psalm 16 made the point that David prophetically described the hope that he would not experience corruption.[327] However, the existence of David's intact tomb indicates that his body had never been raised, and so David could not have been the fulfilment of the prophecy.

Therefore, the Psalm was about the resurrection of the Messiah to which Peter made the important link with bodily existence. Peter declared that Jesus did not remain in the grave and experience corruption - drawing attention to the significance of the bodily resurrection of the person as being central to the hope he was now proclaiming. Jesus did not avoid death, but even though he died, he was raised back to life.[328] Peter's preaching about the defeat of death contrasted by his expectation that David was still in his tomb, helped to explain the nature of *hades*. It was the place of death in which the flesh experienced corruption. It was common experience that what went into the ground

---

[326] Acts 2:29-31
[327] Psalm 16:10 (NKJV)
[328] Acts 2:32-33

began to decay and returned to dust.

There was no sense in Hebrew thought or Peter's preaching that what went into *hades* continued to survive in some form. This is because the expectation was a rescue from the consequences of *hades,* which was the corruption of the flesh. If Hebrew thought suggested the survivability of man in the grave, there would not have been such interest in the physical state of man's condition. What mattered was whether man could be rescued from the grave and the consequent corruption. The resurrection answered this question. It rescued man from death and corruption, returning him to bodily life where there was no corruption.

In Acts 3, a lame man was healed at the gate of the temple, which left the people amazed. Peter once again provided an explanation of the resurrection as the essential proof that death had been defeated and that Jesus was the Messiah. He boldly declared, "You killed the Author of life, whom God raised from the dead."[329] The idea that the Author of life was killed contrasted by the defeat of death, once again pointed to the significance of the resurrection in restoring man to life. In verse 21, Peter stated that the Messiah must remain in heaven until the time of universal restoration, which supports some of the ideas around Paul's teaching of the future timing of the resurrection for the Church.

In Acts 4, the officials were concerned about the

---

[329] Acts 3:15 (NRSV)

people proclaiming in Jesus the resurrection of the Dead. Peter responded by explaining that Jesus Christ of Nazareth whom they had crucified, had indeed been raised from the dead. The theme is repeated in Acts 5, where the Apostles, having been put into prison for preaching the Gospel, were rescued by the Angel of the Lord, then apprehended again, and forced to give an account to the religious leaders. Again, their response was that God had raised Jesus who had been killed.[330]

In Acts 8, Philip preached to the Ethiopian Eunuch whose salvation was based on the sharing of the good news. This was likely to have included the resurrection of the dead, because Philip shared from Isaiah that the Messiah had to die. In Acts 10 there was a man named Cornelius, a centurion of the Italian Cohort who received instructions during an angelic visitation from the Lord to send for Peter. The essential element that Peter shared with Cornelius in explaining the Gospel was that Jesus had died, had been raised on the third day, and he was the judge of the living and the dead. This is a reminder of passages in Revelation where the possibility of life for the just in the first resurrection, is contrasted by the second death for the dead in the second resurrection.

In Acts 13, Paul preached in a Synagogue providing a history lesson that certain prophecies pointed to Jesus. Paul summarized the events leading

---

[330] Acts 5:30-31

up to the crucifixion of Jesus in verses 27-29, and then in verse 30 he stated that God had raised him from the dead, and that for many days he had appeared to the disciples. Again, the essential element of the Christian faith being preached as the Good News was that Jesus had died, and that He had risen from the dead. This Good News of the resurrection of the dead is the transforming power of the Gospel that provides hope. Paul also described the appearance of Jesus before his disciples. The physical return to life was essential evidence of the nature of the resurrection and its defeat of death.

Like Peter, Paul went on to preach from Old Testament prophecies in Psalms. They showed that the promises made to David that he would not experience corruption must have applied to another. This is because after he had "done the will of God in his own generation, he died and was buried with his ancestors, and his body decayed."[331]

Paul explained in the same way as Peter did earlier, that these prophecies did not refer to David, but to the Christ because David had died and his body was corrupted in the grave. This idea was reinforced by Paul's comment in verse 37, which says that when Jesus was raised up by God he experienced no corruption. The idea of corruption being the antithesis of life in the resurrection was a major component of Paul's teaching.

---

[331] Acts 13:36 (NLT)

Paul taught that to avoid corruption there must be a resurrection back to life in a body that is incorruptible. While Jesus was only in the grave for a short time, the degree of corruption that his body might have experienced during that time was not necessarily an issue. The important difference between David and Jesus is that David suffered corruption because he was still in his tomb, whereas Jesus avoided this corruption because of his resurrection.

Peter and Paul both observed that Jesus' body did not suffer corruption in the same way as David, because Jesus had been resurrected back to life. His empty tomb was the proof of this, and demonstrated that death could be defeated and that the body along with the person could be returned to life. There was no suggestion in the Apostle's thinking that the soul survived death, because the emphasis was on avoiding the corruption of the body through the resurrection.

Considering Paul's teaching that we receive *new* incorruptible bodies in the resurrection makes the resurrection of Christ different, because his body did not remain in the grave. However, the nature of Jesus' interaction with the disciples after the resurrection, demonstrated that his body was different. This suggests a resurrection-transformation in line with Paul's understanding of the type of change that occurs to those who are alive at the return of Christ.

While Paul taught that a physical body dies and a spiritual body is raised, we should not become too dogmatic about the difference. While Jesus' body was physical in appearance, it did not necessarily have to obey the laws of nature. "The transformed body is not composed of spirit; it is a body adapted to the eschatological existence that is under the ultimate domination of the Spirit."[332] The promise was that God would transform our lowly body to be like Christ's glorious body.[333] This emphasis on the transformed body in the resurrection is contrary to the belief that man naturally exists beyond the grave as a disembodied entity.

The possibility might be suggested as to whether the *just* that die since Christ's ascension might not immediately be resurrected, avoiding corruption in the same way as Jesus did. However, this would seem to contradict Paul's teaching who expected the Dead to rise at the return of Christ. This idea was reinforced by the fact that as far as the Disciples were concerned, David was still lying corrupted in his tomb after the ascension of Christ. In addition, nowhere afterwards does Paul suggest that David had since been resurrected.

The Apostles emphasis on David's condition of corruption also strongly suggests that they did not believe that David existed as a consciously existing immortal soul. Such an idea would have undermined

---

[332] Gordon Fee, The First Epistle to the Corinthians NICNT (Grand Rapids, MI: Wm. B. Eerdmans, 1987), 786.
[333] Philippians 3:21

the argument being used to support the importance of the bodily resurrection of Christ.

However, a preterist view, which accepts the 'parousia' of Jesus and the resurrection of the dead sometime around the destruction of the Temple in AD70, would mean that from that time, believers immediately receive their new body.[334] Revelation 14:13 might support this… "Blessed are those who die from now on…" Some reject this idea because Paul had rebuked those who believed the resurrection had already occurred. However, because Paul seemed to expect the resurrection in his own lifetime,[335] this would mean that from his perspective it just hadn't happened 'yet'.[336]

In Acts 17, Paul preached to Epicureans and Stoics who were the leading schools of thought among the Greek philosophers. The former group's philosophy of life was one of pleasure and freedom from fear of death. The Stoics held to the high moral principles of a life of self-denial and were pantheists, who believed that nature and God were one. In contrast to Platonic philosophy, the Epicureans did not believe in the immortality of the soul and the Stoics had no clear conception of the afterlife. These philosophers

---

[334] For more information regarding Preterism, The Parousia by James Stuart Russell or The Last Days According to Jesus by R. C. Sproul are useful starting points.
[335] 1 Thessalonians 4:17
[336] This resurrection might have included the elect (Mark 13:20,22,27) and the righteous dead up until that point in time.

were dedicated to debating issues of life and were curious about new ideas.

Paul began explaining to them that God had overlooked times of human ignorance, but that he now commanded everyone to repent, because he had fixed a day of judgment through the man he had appointed. This man was Jesus who had been raised from the dead. However, "When they heard Paul speak about the resurrection of the dead, some laughed in contempt, but others said, "We want to hear more about this later.""[337]

Paul's comments seemed irrational to some, because he was saying that the body mattered, and that life only existed after death when the body was resurrected. However, it is important to note what Paul does not say. There was no mention of the immortality of the soul or any attempt to explain that the judgment involved eternal suffering. Both of these ideas would have had greater appeal to Greek interests, regardless of their philosophical persuasion. Their reaction to Paul's teaching suggests that the resurrection of the body was an uncomfortable idea and contradictory to Greek thought. Therefore, it would be illogical to think that Paul believed in the immortality of the soul, as much as these Greeks believed in the resurrection.

While the Greeks would have been aware of the concept of the resurrection from their own

---

[337] Acts 17:32 (NLT)

mythologies, they certainly did not consider a general resurrection of the dead worthy of attention. However, some were interested enough to hear Paul again on this matter. For some Greeks the possibility of bodily life after death would have been an intriguing possibility, which would ultimately provide a hope that the vague elements of 'soul immortality' could never achieve.

In Acts 23-26, Paul was interrogated by the Pharisees and the Sadducees and then sent to the Roman Authorities. Paul created a division between the two groups by pointing out that he was on trial for the resurrection of the dead.[338] Later on in Acts 26:6-8, he used a similar argument in his discussion with King Agrippa, by complaining that he was on trial for the hope in the promise made to God by his ancestors. Paul's objection to his treatment was based on the argument that his accusers found it incredible that God raises the dead.[339]

In all of these examples, the preaching of the physical resurrection of the dead defined the essential message. Jesus had physically risen from the dead, death had been defeated and those that repent and believe share in the same hope. There was certainly no suggestion that man could naturally circumvent death. There was also no mention of a judgment leading to everlasting torment for the wicked, even though there

---

[338] Acts 23:6-9
[339] Acts 26:8

was plenty of opportunity for Peter and Paul to do so. If the immortality of the soul were part of Paul's theology, he should have appealed to Greek philosophical interests, drawing their attention to similarities between Christianity and Plato's own beliefs. However, Peter and Paul avoided such concepts and consistently and repeatedly reinforced the central aspect of the Christian faith; the belief in a bodily resurrection where Jesus Christ was the firstborn from the dead.

The existence of differing philosophical and religious beliefs contradicts the argument that uniform views negated the need to tell people about everlasting torment. The point is that they did not teach these things, because these ideas were not part of the Gospel message. The important details consistently and repeatedly proclaimed were that death had been defeated, and that Jesus had been raised from the grave.

In his discussions with Felix, Paul described the resurrection of the just and the unjust,[340] and mentioned the coming judgment.[341] However, there was no clear or specific teaching about the nature of these events to suggest that these things proclaimed immortality of the soul or eternal torment. Likewise, in his discussions with the Greeks, Paul merely stated that God had fixed a day in which he would judge the world

---

[340] Acts 24:15
[341] Acts 24:25

in righteousness.[342]

The significance of the resurrection in securing salvation confirms Jesus' repeated statements that whoever believes in him, will live even though they die. How else do we make sense of Paul's words when he says, "If we have been united with him in a death like his, we shall certainly be united with him in a resurrection like his."[343] Paul's hope was always to know Christ and the power of his resurrection through the sharing of his sufferings, that he might somehow like Christ in his death, "Attain the resurrection from the dead."[344]

Paul did not express the hope that he would continue to exist in the afterlife in some form, and then be reunited with his body in the resurrection. Paul's constant expectation was that he would die, and then one day he would come to life in a new body in the resurrection. Tom Wright notes that the word resurrection was never used to describe immediate life after death, but a new bodily life sometime later.[345] The resurrection is a bodily rescue from death and not the avoidance of death. In other words, you cannot have a resurrection without death. The resurrection only happens to dead people and this resurrection occurs sometime after death.[346] In Jewish thought, this was an

---

[342] Acts 17:31
[343] Romans 6:5 (ESV)
[344] Philippians 3:10-11 (NRSV)
[345] Wright, Surprised by Hope, 47
[346] 1 Thessalonians 4:15

end of the age event and therefore Paul deliberately timed the resurrection with the *parousia*. "For as all die in Adam, so all will be made alive in Christ. But each in his own order: Christ the first fruits, then at his coming those who belong to Christ."[347]

---

[347] 1 Corinthians 15:22-23 (NRSV)

# Final Words

We have sought to clarify the nature of man and his potential for future existence. Scripture consistently suggests that man is mortal in nature, and his only hope is in the resurrection of the dead. For some, there can be no possibility of continuous future existence after death. That the unjust cease to exist in the resurrection of condemnation is an idea that may not be popular with some, and we have touched on some of the interpretive issues that might have contributed to the rejection of this idea.

The important thing to remember is that Scripture should define what is important, and that we should not be dogmatic. Dogmatism is often a product of the belief that sees challenges to interpretation, as a challenge to the accuracy of the Bible. It arises from the fear that abandoning a previously held view implies that other beliefs that I might value, are also under some form of threat.

This phenomenon will become extreme when we hold onto beliefs, regardless of whether we have good evidence or not. Our aim therefore was to seek the overall evidence of Scripture to define the potential for man's existence; because correctly understood interpretive principles help to guide us in forming mature and sensible beliefs. What we find is that both the Old and New Testament provide very little evidence for a Hell that is a place of everlasting torment, with the wicked suffering forever and ever.

Central to our argument is the mortality of man. It seems that he does not have immortality, and he is dependent on God to bring him back to life after death in the resurrection. The resurrection is paramount to the Christian faith, because it is the mechanism by which the corruptible will be made incorruptible. If man's immortality is conditional and immortality is immunity from death, then the outcome for the unjust must be death, which Scripture described as an everlasting punishment.

The second death is to be taken seriously. It is described as a punishment of complete destruction. We cannot choose to ignore this idea in the hope that God will allow people to be eternally tormented, just because we believe that such punishment is merited. Grenz for example, who clearly argues against the immortality of the soul,[348] and who supports the importance of the resurrection in granting new life,[349] explained that hell is an expression of the Love of God in the form of wrath. His argument is that God's love is eternal, and it is necessary for the unbeliever to experience that love, albeit under different

---

[348] Grenz, Community of God, 585
[349] Grenz, Community of God, 586

circumstances.[350] However, this idea lacks any clear scriptural basis, and contradicts Jesus' teaching that life was only offered to those who believe. The antithesis of this was always death.

To have everlasting existence is to share the life of God forever in immortal and incorruptible resurrected bodies through the power of God, who is able to bring us back from a place of non-existence. It seems that there can be no such immortality for the unbeliever, because it would be illogical for God to grant immortality merely to punish and torment forever.

There are problems that we may not fully understand, as for example in the nature of the unjust dead in their resurrection. The Bible says that they are dead; they are not souls or persons and their fate is the Lake of Fire, which is the second death. Therefore, it is likely that the wicked are not raised immortal or immune from further death, and their appearance at the judgment must be a temporary event before their final destruction.

Of course, not every question or problem may have been answered. The aim has been to probe the emphasis of Scripture, and use common-sense hermeneutical principles to establish a Biblical perspective of man's potential for future existence. While there are some passages that might appear to

---

[350] Grenz, Community of God, 642

create problems, there are usually interpretative solutions that can be suggested from Scripture. For example, the promise to the penitent criminal on the cross, which seems to suggest that Jesus was offering paradise on the day of their death. "Truly I tell you, today you will be with me in Paradise."[351]

Does this mean that the criminal will survive as an immortal soul and enter with Jesus into paradise on the day of his death to await the resurrection of his body? Paul's description about the timing and the nature of the resurrection would suggest that this passage contradicts previously discussed ideas.

There are also a number of other problems with the idea that the dying criminal is going to enter into paradise on this day. The first problem is that Jesus did not rise from the dead on the day of his death and secondly, there were forty days between his resurrection and his ascension. It is unlikely that the criminal would be following Jesus into paradise, when all these other events had not yet taken place.

Revelation 2:7 described paradise as a reward for those who overcome. The overcomer is the one who despite great uncertainties and difficulties endures persecution to receive the reward of life. Paradise in this context is a reminder of the Garden of Eden, where the Tree of Life is once again offered to man. That which man was banished from is now freely available to those

---

[351] Luke 23:43 (NRSV)

that believe, except the final hurdle of death remains. To the criminal, death would be a sleep from which he would awake into the paradise of the life of God. From his perspective, it would be *today* despite whatever passage of time elapsed between his death, and the eschatological fulfilment of God's purposes.

Even if this argument were incorrect, insisting on an immediate post-mortem existence would severely undermine the significance of the resurrection of Christ. Even the Pharisees knew what Jesus had taught. "Sir, we remember what that impostor said while he was still alive, 'After three days I will rise again.'"[352] While they did not believe what Jesus had said, they knew that his claim implied that he would be dead until his resurrection, because they note that he made this claim while he was "still alive."

In addition to these ideas, Hong notes that there are two ways to translate this verse.[353] In the original Greek, there was no comma between 'today' and 'you' and therefore the text could say, "I tell you today, you will be with me in Paradise." Hong found that the structure of Verb+Today in the Gospels and Acts outnumbers the Today+Verb option, which suggests that moving the comma is a legitimate choice. Therefore, Jesus offered paradise as a future event.

This view would lend weight to Ellis' linguistic

[352] Matthew 27:63 (NRSV)
[353] Joseph Hong, "Understanding and Translating "Today" in Luke 23:43," *The Bible Translator* 46:4 (1995): 408-417, 416

work on the word *today* as a technical expression for the time of messianic salvation.[354] The use of *today* throughout the Gospels and Acts illustrates this hope. For example, "Today this Scripture has been fulfilled in your hearing."[355]

Some might disagree. The counter argument might be that if I ignore the plain meaning of the text, then what can you believe? However, what is the plain meaning of the text? For example, in the story of the Rich Man and Lazarus, should we ignore the fact that this story was likely common folklore, because we prefer to believe that Jesus really wanted us to know what hell was like? To do so we would have to ignore some important issues about context, and the response or lack of response by anyone after concerning the details of this story. Is the plain meaning of the story the background details, or the punch line at the end?

Understanding context and intended meanings are important for interpretation. For example, the Sadducees challenged Jesus on the belief in a resurrection with a hypothetical scenario, in which a woman remarried a number of times upon the death of each of her husbands. Their posing question was who would be her husband in the resurrection. Jesus replied with a quote from the Pentateuch (the Sadducees source of authority) stating, "And as for the

---

[354] Earle E. Ellis, *The Gospel of Luke* (Century Bible New Edition: London: Butler & Tanner, 1974), 268
[355] Luke 4:21 (NRSV)

resurrection of the dead, have you not read what was said to you by God: 'I am the God of Abraham, and the God of Isaac, and the God of Jacob'? He is not God of the dead, but of the living."[356]

From this passage, it might be assumed that Abraham, Isaac and Jacob must have been alive and well. However, because the Sadducees did not believe in the resurrection, Jesus argued that if God is the God of the living then there must be a resurrection. If Jesus were arguing for the immortality of the soul or some type of post mortem/pre-resurrection existence, then that would make nonsense of his argument. This is because the possibility that the dead are enjoying a conscious state of existence negates the importance, or even the need of the resurrection. Therefore, God must be the God of the living because although Abraham was dead, he would not remain dead forever and would live again...in the resurrection.

These ideas are reinforced by Jesus himself in the very same passage, when he explains the relationship between death and the resurrection in a future age. "Those who are considered worthy of a place *in that age* and in the resurrection from the dead ...cannot die anymore, because they are like angels and are children of God, being children of the resurrection."[357]

Other passages like that in Acts 7:59, where

---

[356] Matthew 22:31-32 (ESV)
[357] Luke 20:35-36 (NRSV)

Stephen commits his spirit to the Lord, need to be interpreted in conjunction with an understanding of idiomatic expressions. Stephen's spirit was not about to depart his body, but rather his life was being entrusted to God's care until the resurrection. We have already seen how the breath/spirit that returns to God at death is a metaphorical expression of the life that God gives.

Ambiguous passages like James 4:5 do not really help to explain the nature of man. Depending on which translation is used, the verse can refer to either the spirit of man or the Spirit. Does it say, "The Spirit who dwells in us yearns jealously"[358] or "God yearns jealously for the spirit that he has made to dwell in us?"[359]

Sound theology is always built on the emphasis of Scripture, and difficult or ambiguous passages require careful consideration of a wider context. So, when Paul says that to be absent from the body is to be with the Lord,[360] we should also note what he had stated a few verses prior. He said that when his earthly house - his tent, was destroyed, he had a building from God - a habitation from heaven in which he would be clothed, and that he would not be found naked.

When Paul says he would not be found naked, he meant that he would not be a disembodied soul, as in Greek contemporary thought. Therefore, to be absent from the body idiomatically describes death, and the

---

[358] NKJV
[359] NRSV
[360] 2 Corinthians 5:8

expression to be with the Lord is the hope that death is like a sleep, where the passage of time until the resurrection is of no importance. Regardless of the terminology of death, Scripture still expects that the return to life will require a bodily form.

Correct interpretive principles suggest that man's rebellion against God resulted in a loss of existence. This loss of existence is called death, which God defined as the dissolution of the body, which makes him a mortal being. If we ignore the extensive teaching on the mortality of man that we must put on immortality in the resurrection, then we might be able to believe that man is naturally immortal, and will continue to exist in death.

However, the idea of an immortal being is contradictory to the role of the *Pneuma* of God in providing life. If man is already immortal, then he automatically and independently advances into the afterlife. The belief that man is naturally immortal also suggests that Satan was correct, when he told Eve that she would not really die. However, since Satan is the father of lies,[361] it is more likely that the reverse is true.

Jesus' teaching stated that those that believed in him would live, even if they died,[362] which suggests that those who do not believe will die, or remain dead. Therefore, immortality must be conditional on that

---

[361] John 8:44
[362] John 11:26

belief, an idea that was frequently reinforced by Jesus himself. He said to the Pharisees that they would die in their sins if they did not believe in him, and they would not be able to go where he was going.[363] They could not follow him, because that involved a resurrection into an immortal life in a new body, and this was only promised to those that believe.

These ideas are confirmed by passages such as that made in Isaiah 26:14, which described the enemies of God's people. "They are dead, they will not live; They are deceased, they will not rise."[364] While this might seem to contradict scriptures that indicate a resurrection of condemnation for the unjust, the word rise (*qum*) can mean endure or continue. So, this verse could say they (the wicked) are dead, they will not continue. This nuance is exemplified in 1 Samuel 13:14, where Saul is told that his kingdom would not continue (*qum*).

Therefore, while the unjust might rise in the resurrection of condemnation, they will not endure (rise or stand up under) the judgment, and will not live. This idea is strengthened by comparing verse 19 of the same chapter, where Isaiah assured his faithful peers that *their* dead *will* rise (*qum*) in the resurrection.

While our aim was to rely on Scripture, there is still some room for philosophical reflection. For

---

[363] John 8:21-24
[364] Isaiah 26:14 (NKJV)

example, the concept of a naturally immortal being means that man will continue to exist after death. Besides the obvious theological issues, this idea would seem to make the resurrection an unusual, secondary or redundant event. If we consider this existence as a conscious experience in a pre-resurrection state, then why would an immortal being that is enjoying the afterlife require a body? Would it not also be easier to assign a new body immediately after death? As an alternative, a non-conscious state of existence might be closer to the truth, but there are still problems. How can I be immortal and yet unconscious...how does an immortal soul become unconscious? Of course, these questions do not require an answer. The Biblical picture of the resurrection of the dead by the power of God seems a sufficient solution.

If man was created as an immortal being, then the wicked must also exist forever. This would mean that the post mortem existence of the wicked would require a judgment, leading to a punishment that is described by some as everlasting torment. If we choose to accept this idea, then we have to consider the moral problems with a God who consigns people to hell. As long as the human population continues in its current state, there would be an increasing number of people who find themselves in eternal torment. Should God allow the current circumstances to continue, knowing that his inaction is increasing the possibility of greater suffering and torment?

We would also have to consider the problem of living in God's kingdom knowing that there are others, who are suffering for eternity. Would we be satisfied living in a universe knowing that granny was swimming around in a lake of fire?[365] These problems do not suggest that the moral problem is the only argument against eternal torment. The point, as we have already seen, is that these ideas are contrary to the view presented by scripture.

Then there are the problems around the idea of an immortal soul as a divisible part of man. If man is a divisible being then what is the soul and what is its metaphysical makeup? If it separates from me in death, would it be the real me? If it is the real me, then what function did all those physical, neurological connections in the brain serve?

Is it possible that there are two of me? One *me* that is an expression of the activity of the neurological connections in the brain and *me* that is a soul? If there are two of *me*, then which one is the real *me*? By that I mean, which part is the thinking, feeling, self-determinate being, which is self-aware of his existence. They cannot both be that, because it does not seem possible that I could exist as two beings that operate separately, and yet are both accountable to God as one.

---

[365] This might be considered the stereotypical view and some might find it necessary to moderate or spiritualize the nature of this eternal suffering. Regardless, the natural immortality of the soul supports the concept of an everlasting punishment.

The difficulty with the idea of a dualistic nature is that if the immortal soul is understood to be distinct from the body, then it must in essence be separate from the self that exists as a function of physiological processes. Grenz summarizes the critic's view of this dualism, as an emphasis on an immaterial soul, leading to an unbiblical deprecation of the body.[366] Consequently, the problems generated by these anthropological issues leads Grenz himself to conclude, that our "essential nature is holistic...the human person is by divine design one indivisible reality."[367]

Because of these conflicting views over anthropological identity, it is more likely that the soul is actually the expression of the physical connections that exist in the brain. It might be possible that in death, when the brain stops functioning, the essential self defined by those physical connections lives on unaffected by death. However, this idea contradicts the close connection between the body and immortality described by Paul. Immortality was a direct function of the self, raised from death in a new spiritually engineered and incorruptible body. Because Scripture suggests that *zoe* life only exists if there is going to be a body or a container for the self, then it makes sense that this will be the new body we receive in the resurrection.

However, this does not mean that the self

---

[366] Grenz, Community of God, 159
[367] Grenz, Community of God, 163

naturally survives waiting for this event. The self survives because God remembers us, and it is the power of God that recalls us back into existence, as we simultaneously receive our new bodies. Therefore, the soul seems to be us, as we know ourselves. The complete us including emotions, desires, expectations, memories, hopes and dreams. I am defined by all these things physically expressed through the neurological functions of the brain. My body will return to dust, but God knows and remembers me and can reinstate me in a new body.

Paul was also careful to note the link between our resurrection and the state of creation. Through sin, Creation was cursed and subject to futility,[368] which meant that it was unable to achieve its goal or purpose. Although we have focussed on how death affects man, all of creation is subject to some form of decay. The second Law of Thermodynamics explains that everything ultimately falls apart and disintegrates over time. Many animals are specialised killers also subject to death, disorder, and chaos. In addition, storms, earthquakes, and volcanism along with disease bring devastation to lives and communities.

While the original purpose of creation was made futile by sin, God allowed this subjection to futility in the hope that the creation itself would be set free from

---

[368] Romans 8:19 NRSV

174

its bondage to decay.[369] Paul linked this freedom from bondage to decay with the resurrection, which in turn supports Scripture's idea of a new heaven and a new earth.[370] Therefore, the whole universe is *groaning* in anticipation of freedom from decay. This freedom will occur when the children of God receive their inheritance, which is the redemption of their bodies.

Although Paul talked about waiting for the redemption of a body,[371] he was not talking about immortal souls waiting for the resurrection. The language was inclusive of himself and others who were still alive. They were groaning inwardly for the time when the bondage to decay was finally extinguished in the resurrection. He could not escape the conclusion that our existence is intrinsically linked with the survival of the body, because it is when our bodies are restored that we begin to experience *zoe* life.

These ideas explain that the corruption of the universe, occurring because of man's disobedience, can only end at the physical resurrection of the dead. The corruptible will put on the incorruptible, and this will happen in the final consummation of all things.

While man requires a solution for death, Scripture suggests that sin and death co-exist as the problem. The idea that sin leads to death is equivalent with the corruption that leads to decay is the persistent

---

[369] Romans 8:19-23
[370] Isaiah 65:17
[371] Romans 8:23

message of Scripture. Sin leads to death, but salvation through Christ's atoning work on the cross leads to everlasting life.

Scripture is clear about these things. We are all disobedient creatures cursed to return to the dust from where we came. However, that curse has been overcome through the second Adam, who gave his life by dying on a cross for the forgiveness of sin and in doing so, defeated the power of death. It is through the same power that raised Jesus from the dead that we live in hope of a new, incorruptible, and immortal existence in God's kingdom for all eternity.

To ignore some of the ideas discussed in this book, suggests that we should dogmatically continue to insist on the idea of a fiery hell for the unbeliever for all eternity. Such dogmatism also creates its own unique and additional problems. For example, Universalism - the argument that states that all will be eventually saved - probably owes its existence to those who reject the thought of a hell and can find no suitable alternative.

Misunderstood ideas about the Christian faith will continue to perpetuate stereotypical assumptions. For some, the fear of Hell does not reinforce the image of a loving God, while Universalism weakens the seriousness of sin and man's rebellion against God.

Conditional immortality solves these sorts of problems. The resurrection of the dead is the key truth that links much of Scripture into a unified whole. Jesus died to deal with the problem of death and he left us with the promise of the resurrection. It is the promise of eternal life in a new body.

There is a message to pass on. Death has been conquered! In Jesus, we receive forgiveness for our sins and share in the resurrection to eternal life. While all of this should be good news to most, bringing people to a place where they can accept this message remains a challenge. In general, most in the western world live in relatively good health. Death may not hold the same power in the minds of those who are assured by modern medical interventions, and the promise of scientific advance. Most also live in comfort and wealth unheard of in times past. The stereotypical view of a Christian belief in judgment, which results in unbelievers being hurtled into everlasting torment, will certainly not help direct people to the real issues.

This does not mean that we should neglect what Scripture has to say about judgment. The Bible specifically states that there will be a judgment, and for some the end is a second death. Therefore, we should remember the words of Jesus, who told us to enter through the narrow gate, "For the gate is wide and the road is easy that leads to destruction, and there are many who take it."[372]

---

[372] Matthew 7:13-14 NRSV

# Index

Printed in Great Britain
by Amazon

22325979R00118